Audio, Video and Media *in* the Ministry

DR. CLARENCE FLOYD RICHMOND
Author

D1548465

THOMAS NELSON
Since 1798

NASHVILLE   DALLAS   MEXICO CITY   RIO DE JANEIRO

Published in Nashville, TN, by Thomas Nelson.
Thomas Nelson is a trademark of Thomas Nelson, Inc.

Thomas Nelson, Inc., titles may be purchased in bulk for educational, business, fund-raising, or sales promotional use. For information, please email: SpecialMarkets@ThomasNelson.com

Book Interior: Stephen Ramirez

Editor: Gabriel Hernandez

Technical Editor: Dan Wothke

Series Editor: Michael Lawson

Produced in Association with Lawson Music Media, Inc.

Library of Congress Cataloging-in-Publication Data is available upon request.

ISBN: 1418541745

ISBN-13: 9781418541743

Printed in the United States of America

1 2 3 4 5 6 7 8 — 13 12 11 10

Contents

CONTENTS

CONTENTS

Foreword

AUDIO, VIDEO AND MEDIA HANDBOOK FOR CHURCH VOLUNTEERS

In a worship service a great measure of responsibility rests on those who volunteer in the audio, video, and media ministries. When everything is going well, no one notices; but when the microphones don't work or feedback creeps into the service, when the sound is too loud or the projected lyrics are late, everyone does. A well functioning audio, video, and media team can help the congregation enter into a deeper and more meaningful worship. A team that doesn't anticipate or prevent problems, and react when they arise, is a distraction instead. This handbook serves as a guide for those beginning to work in this ministry. It's goal is to help volunteers function to the top of their ability and contribute positively to a successful worship service.

TOPICS WILL INCLUDE

- Common areas of AV audio-video ministry including, sound, projection, lighting, audio and video, broadcast, and Web;
- Equipment that will be encountered;
- Selection, setup, operation, storage, and maintenance of that equipment;
- Common problems in rehearsals and in services, and strategies for preventing and solving them, and;
- Working with the pastors, musicians, ministry leaders, and the congregation.

While this book won't turn a new volunteer into an instant audio engineer, it will help them understand how important they are to the ministry, and how to support the seasoned volunteers and professionals trusted with the production of worship services.

CHAPTER 1

Introduction

OPEN LETTER TO MEDIA TEAM MEMBERS

Dear Media Team Member,

Welcome to our team. Your work in the media ministry at our church is greatly appreciated and will make a significant difference in the quality of our church's worship and the scope of our ministry.

Today's church members are often media-centric. They attend movies, watch hundreds of channels on television, spend hours on the Internet, and download music and video to their phones and other personal media devices. With this increased exposure to media comes an expectation that the quality of music and media that they encounter in churches and worship will be exemplary. The goal of the media team is to meet those expectations, to deepen the worship experience, and to broaden the ministry of our church. In this effort we partner with our pastors, music ministers, and other ministries within the church. In many ways our role is one of service and support. In this we are following the example set by Christ

(Philippians 2: 5-8). Also, lest anyone forget, there is no member of the body of Christ that does not perform an essential function (1 Corinthians 12:12-27). Your unique contributions are essential to our worship and other services, and to our outreach as a whole. Thank you for your ministry and service.

Sincerely,
Your Media Team Coordinator

SCRIPTURES FOR STUDY

Let this mind be in you which was also in Christ Jesus, who, being in the form of God, did not consider it robbery to be equal with God, but made Himself of no reputation, taking the form of a bondservant, and coming in the likeness of men. And being found in appearance as a man, He humbled Himself and became obedient to the point of death, even the death of the cross.

Philippians 2:5-8

For as the body is one and has many members, but all the members of that one body, being many, are one body, so also is Christ. For by one Spirit we were all baptized into one body—whether Jews or Greeks, whether slaves or free—and have all been made to drink into one Spirit. For in fact the body is not one member but many.

If the foot should say, "Because I am not a hand, I am not of the body," is it therefore not of the body? And if the ear should say, "Because I am not an eye, I am not of the body," is it therefore not of the body? If the whole body were an eye, where would be the hearing? If the whole were hearing, where would be the smelling? But now God has set the members, each one of them, in the body just as He pleased. And if they were all one member, where would the body be? But now indeed there are many members, yet one body. And the eye cannot say to the hand, "I have no need of you"; nor again the head to the feet, "I have no need of you." No, much rather, those members of the body which seem to be weaker are necessary. And those members of the body which we think to be less honorable, on these we bestow greater honor; and our unpresentable parts have greater modesty, but our presentable parts have no need. But God composed the body, having given greater honor to that part which lacks it, that there should be no schism in the body, but that the members should have the same care for one another. And if one member suffers, all the members suffer with it; or if one member is honored, all the members rejoice with it.

Now you are the body of Christ, and members individually.

1 Corinthians 12:12-30

PURPOSE

This book is intended to serve as a guide to help churches achieve success in the ministry of audio, video, and media. The first two chapters contain an introduction and explanation of the organization and maintenance of the ministry. The remaining chapters are devoted to the technical aspects including the basics of sound reinforcement, video projection, lighting, recording and editing audio and video, broadcasting, Web development, and network maintenance. Each chapter has a checklist, which can be used by the media ministry leader, distributed to ministry team members, or customized for specific needs within the church. Each chapter has a troubleshooting section that will help solve many of the problems that will be encountered in the media ministry. Each chapter also has a discussion of the function, setup, care, and maintenance of relevant equipment.

IMPORTANCE OF THE MEDIA MINISTRY TEAM

The importance of the media team in enhancing the church's ministry cannot be overstated. Without sound amplification or reinforcement, members of the congregation may not be able to hear what is being said thereby missing important material. Without a microphone, preachers or presenters in a large space could lose their voice, long before their message is complete. Without appropriate equipment, the quality of the music may drive people away from worship rather than draw them into it. In many of today's churches worship songs come and go rapidly and printed materials cannot be produced quickly enough. Without projection of lyrics, people will find it more difficult to worship. Without audio and video examples, many sermon points will fall flat. Without a recording or broadcast ministry, many may not hear of God's great love.

But ta-da, enter the audio and video ministry team. With a well-honed media ministry, these, and many more pitfalls can be avoided. With a healthy media ministry, the congregation can hear and understand the proclamation of the word of God; preachers and presenters can speak with ease, even when their voices are weak; the worship music may be enhanced so that it is more attractive and people can draw closer to God; the lyrics of each song can be projected and the people can truly sing a new song unto the Lord; and many sermon points can be visually illustrated so that they are both easier to understand and more memorable. With a properly functioning media team, the equipment which makes these things possible can be maintained, and used to its fullest advantage, the distractions produced by audio feedback can be avoided, the volume of the music can be set to a comfortable level, and worship can be enhanced. With an active media team and recording or broadcast ministry, the reach of the church can be expanded and the kingdom of God can be built.

IT'S ABOUT SERVICE

There is no ministry in the church that is not ultimately about service. The pastor, though in a leadership role, must have a servant's heart to be successful. The shepherd's job may be mistaken for a position of power. Actually, it is one of service and responsibility to the sheep (the congregation). The shepherd must gather the sheep into the flock and keep them from getting lost. If one is lost, the shepherd must find and rescue it. The shepherd must find green pastures where the sheep may safely feed. He must find clean water to quench the thirst of their flock. The shepherd must keep the sheep safe from the wolves and bears, bind their wounds, and nourish the lame and sick. The goals of the church are the same. God does not desire that any should perish. He longs for all to come to know Christ, to be filled with His Holy Spirit, and to grow and mature spiritually. Much of this is accomplished by the ministry of the church's servant-leaders, not just the pastors. As a member of the audio, video, and media ministry, you are a part of that servant leadership.

A SCRIPTURAL FOUNDATION FOR SERVICE

God has a unique plan for every individual and their contribution to building His kingdom. That plan includes many positions, but the Holy Spirit directs each.

> *Now concerning spiritual gifts, brethren, I do not want you to be ignorant: You know that you were Gentiles, carried away to these dumb idols, however you were led. Therefore I make known to you that no one speaking by the Spirit of God calls Jesus accursed, and no one can say that Jesus is Lord except by the Holy Spirit. There are diversities of gifts, but the same Spirit. There are differences of ministries, but the same Lord. And there are diversities of activities, but it is the same God who works all in all. But the manifestation of the Spirit is given to each one for the profit of all: for to one is given the word of wisdom through the Spirit, to another the word of knowledge through the same Spirit, to another faith by the same Spirit, to another gifts of healings by the same Spirit, to another the working of miracles, to another prophecy, to another discerning of spirits, to another different kinds of tongues, to another the interpretation of tongues. But one and the same Spirit works all these things, distributing to each one individually as He wills.*
>
> **1 Corinthians 12:1-11**

The teachings of Christ contain many examples of service. When Jesus said that the first shall be last and the last, first, it is immediately followed by an explanation of the seeming contradiction of His servant leadership.

So the last will be first, and the first last. For many are called, but few chosen." Now Jesus, going up to Jerusalem, took the twelve disciples aside on the road and said to them, "Behold, we are going up to Jerusalem, and the Son of Man will be betrayed to the chief priests and to the scribes; and they will condemn Him to death, and deliver Him to the Gentiles to mock and to scourge and to crucify. And the third day He will rise again."

Matthew 20:16-19

According to Christ, the Gentiles lord their position over those beneath them. Christians, however, are not to do so.

Then the mother of Zebedee's sons came to Him with her sons, kneeling down and asking something from Him. And He said to her, "What do you wish?" She said to Him, "Grant that these two sons of mine may sit, one on Your right hand and the other on the left, in Your kingdom." But Jesus answered and said, "You do not know what you ask. Are you able to drink the cup that I am about to drink, and be baptized with the baptism that I am baptized with?" They said to Him, "We are able." So He said to them, "You will indeed drink My cup, and be baptized with the baptism that I am baptized with; but to sit on My right hand and on My left is not Mine to give, but it is for those for whom it is prepared by My Father." And when the ten heard it, they were greatly displeased with the two brothers. But Jesus called them to Himself and said, "You know that the rulers of the Gentiles lord it over them, and those who are great exercise authority over them. Yet it shall not be so among you; but whoever desires to become great among you, let him be your servant. And whoever desires to be first among you, let him be your slave—just as the Son of Man did not come to be served, but to serve, and to give His life a ransom for many."

Matthew 20:20-28

THE DISCIPLES ARGUE ABOUT GREATNESS

Now there was also a dispute among them, as to which of them should be considered the greatest. And He said to them, "The kings of the Gentiles exercise lordship over them, and those who exercise authority over them are called 'benefactors.' But not so among you; on the contrary, he who is greatest among you, let him be as the younger, and he who governs as he who serves.

Luke 22:24-26

Jesus set a high standard for service by washing his disciple's feet. He showed great humility, and by doing so, he taught his disciples that they should serve one another in the same manner.

So when He had washed their feet, taken His garments, and sat down again, He said to them:

"Do you know what I have done to you? You call Me Teacher and Lord, and you say well, for so I am. If I then, your Lord and Teacher, have washed your feet, you also ought to wash one another's feet. For I have given you an example, that you should do as I have done to you.

John 13:12-15

Christ did not come to be served, but to serve. He gave the perfect model of service in His sacrifice on the cross, and challenged us to do the same.

Then Jesus said to His disciples, "If anyone desires to come after Me, let him deny himself, and take up his cross, and follow Me.

Matthew 16:24

Our job is to serve Christ to the best of our ability. With the correct heart for service, the goals of the media ministry can be achieved.

CHAPTER 2

Media Team Organization and Oversight

In a small church it may be possible for one person to do much of the work associated with the media ministry. As the size of the church increases, however, it is desirable to incorporate more volunteers in this ministry, and consequently, there is a great need for an organized approach.

Churches throughout the world vary in both type and size. Although it is impossible for each one to organize their media ministries in the same way, some principles apply from the smallest to the largest churches. All, regardless of size, will need to create a plan for applying these principles within their media ministries.

THE MEDIA COORDINATOR

First, there needs to be someone who has responsibility for the media ministry. This person should have technical skills, a servant's heart, and a vision for the media ministry. They should be able to handle criticism well, work within an environment where conflicting signals are sometimes received, be an effective communicator, and be flexible.

MEDIA COORDINATOR RESPONSIBILITIES

The responsibilities of the media coordinator include:

- Research and purchase the equipment needed for the various ministries of the church.
- Prepare a budget each year for the maintenance and replacement of equipment used in the church.
- Set up the equipment for the most efficient operation.
- Execute the necessary maintenance each year on existing equipment.
- Recruit members for the various media positions described below.
- Train or plan training for members for the various media positions described below.
- Prepare instructions and checklists for the various media positions described below.
- Critique each service for strengths and weaknesses in the media ministry and address problems so that they are less likely to occur in the future.
- Coordinate media personnel for various services and special events.
- Coordinate media personnel for various spaces in the church.
- Work cooperatively with various church ministries requiring media support, especially the music ministry.
- Secure the necessary licensing for broadcast, Web streaming, projection of lyrics, etc. Make certain that the individuals who work in these areas are aware of licensing limitations and take the necessary precautions to avoid violating them. Do any necessary reporting of copyright usage.
- Secure permissions from any individuals who are being broadcast or whose images are being used in the church's Web pages.
- Oversee a system for providing backup strategies for failed equipment and be available to assist in implementing those plans.

WORKING WITH THE PASTOR

It is important that the media coordinator understand their relationship to the pastor, who oversees all ministries within a church. In the day-to-day operations of the church, the pastor is the final authority on any matters of dispute. Typically the pastor, however, is someone who presents a vision and explains goals and then leaves the details of their implementation to those most directly involved in the ministry. The Pastor, however, will be a great ally as his or her role in leadership includes the responsibility to make certain that the materials and resources to do an effective job are available. The media coordinator will have to work through issues related to the budget with the pastor and/or others designated for that purpose.

BUDGET

Budget is a primary concern for a successful media ministry. A media ministry depends heavily on equipment. When that equipment breaks down, it needs to be repaired or replaced immediately—in time for the next service. The media coordinator should develop a budget for required maintenance on existing equipment and its replacement at the end of its life cycle. The media coordinator will need to spend a great deal of time researching specifications as the budget is developed. Caution must be used to find objective advice. An outside consultant who is not a salesman can often give balanced advice, more so than someone who has a vested interest in the product being considered. Be on guard if salesmen suggest that whoever did the previous installation didn't know what they were doing. While this is sometimes true, it's very likely that equipment acquired in the past was well-advised at the time. The world of media is not one that is marked clearly with road signs indicating what will work and what will not. There will be some perfectly good solutions that may not work as well as hoped in specific installations. Guard against salesmen who do the following:

- Try to establish their expertise at the expense of competitors or those doing previous installations.

- Try to pressure purchase decisions.
- Imposes deadlines on special prices.

TIPS FOR DEALING WITH SALESMEN

- Ask for references and call those people with whom they previously worked.
- Find out how happy their previous customers are with their purchases.
- Visit the churches where other installations occurred and check the results.

LOOK FOR CONSULTANTS WHO DO THE FOLLOWING

- Establish expertise by references.
- Present multiple options with pros and cons of each.

Consultants, unlike salesmen, are usually paid for their services independent of purchasing decisions.

DOUBLE PURPOSING EQUIPMENT

One's philosophical approach to budgeting should also receive consideration. It is possible to do much ministry with basic equipment including some that may be borrowed or donated, or double purposed (for example, a computer may serve as a projection unit on Sunday, but be used for secretarial work the rest of the week), BUT this invites a greater number of problems for both purposes. Ideally the equipment for the ministry should be devoted to that purpose. A computer used in the media ministry should meet the necessary specifications. For example, two video cards are generally needed for use with most projection software. A secretary's computer seldom has the need for such a feature. As quality equipment is acquired for the ministry and is devoted specifically for that purpose, problems decrease.

THE MEDIA MINISTRY ORGANIZATION

While the Pastor's role is clear, it is quite possible that any number of other individuals may be found in the organizational structure of a given church. These individuals will often include music ministers, worship leaders, choir and orchestra directors, associate pastors, and so on. Regardless, it is likely that there will be a person in charge of music ministries. Whether this person is seen as the supervisor of media ministries or a colleague will depend much on the strengths, ages, tenure, and philosophies of individuals in the church itself. It might also depend on whether the church has a significant recording and distribution ministry, broadcast ministry, or if the activities of the media department are directed more toward the worship services within the church. A few common organizational strategies are found below.

These organizational structures are to facilitate the smooth operation of the ministries with one another. It is wise to have a clear understanding of these to help avoid conflicts.

1	2		3				
Board of Deacons or Elders	Board of Deacons or Elders		Board of Deacons or Elders				
PASTOR	PASTOR		PASTOR				
Music Minister	Music Minister	Media Coordinator	Assoc Pastor 1	Assoc Pastor 2		etc.	
Media Coordinator			Music	Media	Children	Youth	etc.

For example, let's say that a worship leader has, in rehearsal, established volume levels for each song. If someone in the congregation walks by and comments that things are too loud, it is important to respectfully receive their input, check with the worship leader (if and when practical) and adjust if possible, and perhaps direct the congregant to a quieter spot in the auditorium until adjustments can be made. If the pastor comments that the music is too loud, there may need to be a different course of action. Even so, everyone must display a spirit of teamwork and support. It is essential that all are working toward the same goals, and that a spirit of cooperation and unity are in place.

WORKING WITH MUSICIANS

Of the various relationships with ministry leaders, it is essential that the media coordinator have a good rapport with those in the music ministry. Most musicians have a good idea of how they would like things to sound. Also, they are able to consider whether someone in the ensemble needs more or less amplification based on musical goals. Ideally, they are acutely aware of whose tone blends well, who sings in or out-of-tune, etc. A sound technician will hopefully have these skills also, but it is important to listen carefully to the instructions from the musicians.

Even so, the experience and background of the musicians vary greatly. Many are trained to better understand an acoustic environment. Opera singers sing the way they do because opera came of age in a day when amplification was not available. Singers had to produce the biggest (loudest) and most beautiful sounds possible with only their voices. In today's churches we are often blessed by operatic voices, but with amplification, we can also enjoy softer voices. The point, however is that trained musicians often have a background in acoustic music and their vocabulary and expectations may reflect that. Younger musicians may have worked more with amplified music and have greater facility in that area, but they too will need support for successful ministry. The number of ways that a sound system can be set up or a platform can be organized is infinite. Any musician stepping onto the platform will require some explanation of how the systems in this space work, where inputs are located, what monitor controls are available on the platform (if any), etc. Supporting the musicians, regardless of their experience in sound reinforcement, in the production of the best musical performance possible is the goal.

THE MEDIA MINISTRY TASKS

The Media Coordinator is likely to oversee a number of important tasks. A list of basic items is found below.

- Sound reinforcement for the worship service, youth service, children's service, singles service, other services, and special events, etc.

- Projection for all of the above.
- Audio recording of some or all of the above.
- Video recording of some or all of the above.
- Lighting for all of the above.
- Editing and preparation of the recordings for broadcast or Internet streaming.
- Oversight of the church's Website.
- Maintenance of computer networks within the church including network disks, printers, servers, etc.

The more of these responsibilities that a Media Coordinator has, the less likely it is that one person can do them all. It will be necessary to mobilize a team of volunteers to help with these tasks.

KEEP IT SIMPLE

Consequently, the media coordinator will find it helpful to setup equipment in a way so that individuals with light training can operate it, and so that it can quickly be put into service. There will be more about this in the technical chapters, but here, suffice it to say, there are numerous examples of how operations can become more complicated than necessary.

EXAMPLE 1: In one service that I oversee, I prepare the projection slides in advance and have a member of the group step into service with few instructions other than, "Type the right arrow to go forward and the left arrow to go backward." This group is small and there is no one in it who could do the entire preparation for the projection, but by keeping operation simple, I can easily find volunteers to do the part they can.

EXAMPLE 2: In one building we have an electronic keyboard which serves as a controller for a much better sound module. Unfortunately because of the use of the space, this keyboard must be set up and put away each week. While using the keyboard and controller gives us access to a broader palette of sounds, the reconnection of MIDI cables and power to all devices, is much more complicated and trouble-prone than setting up a keyboard with built-in sounds. Most of the time this system is used, the person using it plays only the electronic piano sound, so a much less expensive solution would have been equally functional. Of course, training the keyboardist to use the gear to a greater extent would also be possible, but again, the principle is to keep things simple.

Also, there are many instances when "plug and play" operation would be possible, but because of flaws in the design process or equipment acquisition, there is significant setup required instead. Of course, the extra setup is sometimes worthwhile, especially when the quality is significantly enhanced. Even so, when setup becomes more complex, it also becomes more difficult to find volunteers who can step into the position when vacations and other conflicts inevitably occur.

Generally it is best in a church environment to have equipment that is easy to operate and which does not require extensive training.

MEDIA TEAM ORGANIZATION

Ideally there will be at least one person in charge of each of the areas of media ministry. Descriptions of each of their responsibilities are found below.

Sound Reinforcement

For every worship service, there should be a person in charge of sound reinforcement. Duties of this position will include the following:

- Attendance and setup for any rehearsals for the service.
- Turning on equipment as needed for rehearsal.
- Take notes during rehearsal on what is needed for each part of the service. The regular worship service becomes routine but special services will require greater attention and preparation.
- Turning off and putting away equipment as needed after the rehearsal.
- Turning on equipment as needed for the service.
- Attendance and setup for the service.
- Attentive execution of the plans rehearsed previously.
- Turning off and putting away equipment as needed after the service.

Projection

For every worship service, there should be a separate person in charge of projection. Duties of this position will include the following:

Before the Rehearsal

- Secure the list of songs for the service and enter or download them into the projection software.

- Get copies of any DVDs, computer videos, announcements, promotional PowerPoints, or other media to be displayed and prepare them for presentation.
- Get copies of sermon notes and/or outlines, Bible verses, or other information to be displayed and enter them into the projection software.
- Place screens, turn on projectors, etc.
- If video from a live feed will be projected, there should be one or more camera operators and perhaps a video production team providing that signal. Check to make certain the signal for the live feed is active.

At Rehearsal

- Run through the entire service making notes about anything out of the ordinary. Again, regular services become routine, but special services require greater preparation.
- Power down and put away any equipment as needed after the service.

The Service

- Place screens, turn on projectors, etc.
- Double check to see that everything is ready.
- Double check the "order of service" to make certain nothing has changed.
- Attentively execute the plans as rehearsed.
- Afterward, power down and put away equipment as needed.
- File (or delete) any records of the service as needed.

Audio Recording

Recording audio can be as simple as adding a recording device to the soundboard, or as complex as routing signals from a digital mixing board into a virtual mixer on a computer. The chapter on audio recording and editing will present additional options. Depending on the solution selected the responsibilities of someone in this position could vary greatly. The simplest solutions could be added to the responsibility of the sound reinforcement person. The more complex solutions would require a dedicated person on this task. Regardless, the responsibilities of this position will include the following:

- Power on any necessary equipment for recording.
- Place the media for recording in the recording equipment.
- Check the signal levels coming into the recording equipment and set them appropriately.
- Start and stop the recording at the appropriate times in the service.
- Press the "marker" button for each section of the service, if required by the recording equipment.
- Depending on the solution used for recording, mixing may or may not be necessary, and could occur either at this time, or after the recording is complete.
- After the service, save the recording, or finalize any media as needed (burn to CDs, etc.).
- After any necessary editing, provide copies of the service in an appropriate format to the person or persons in charge of broadcast or Web services, and file a copy in the church's archives.
- Make copies of the media for those who request or purchase a copy of the service.
- Power down any equipment as necessary.

Video Recording

Video recording is also possible on any number of levels. In a simple circumstance, a single camera can be directed toward the platform to record the service and can be used to record video and audio concurrently. The use of multiple cameras, as discussed in the chapter on video recording can be used to produce a higher quality video recording. Adding a sound track that was recorded and edited in post-production also increases the quality of the video recording. Minimally the following duties will be required of the person or persons in charge of video recording:

- Power on any cameras and necessary equipment for recording.
- If required by the camera, make any adjustments necessary for white balance.
- If the recording is to take place in a camera, check to confirm that the media for recording is in the camera. If the capacity of the media will be exceeded during the service, make certain that additional media is on hand.
- If the signal from the camera is being directed to a mixing board then check the signal from the camera to the mixing board, and check to make certain that any software or hardware is appropriately configured for recording.
- If multiple cameras are being used, check the communication system between the producer and the camera operators.

- Start recording once the service is in progress. If multiple cameras are being used, camera operators should follow the directions of the "producer."
- Depending on the solution used for recording, mixing may or may not be necessary, and could occur either at this time, or after the recording is complete.
- After the service, save the recording, or finalize any media as needed (burn to DVD).
- After any necessary editing, provide copies of the service in an appropriate format to the person or persons in charge of broadcast or Web services, and file a copy in the church's archives.
- Make copies of the media for those who request or purchase a copy of the service.
- Power down any equipment as necessary.

Lighting

One element that is often overlooked in church services is the application of lighting to enhance the service. Greater attention is typically given to lighting during special programs such as musicals and dramas. Ideally, there will be a system of lights wired into a control board which can be operated by an individual. The use of spotlights will require additional personnel, and as productions increase in complexity, the personnel required to execute the lighting plan will increase. The lighting team also typically handles special effects such as bubbles, fog, snow, etc. Minimally, the following will be necessary for lighting:

- Review the service with the person in charge well in advance of the service. Lighting may sometimes require special placement of fixtures, wiring enhancements, or the building of lighting "sets." In some cases, additional equipment (extra spots) may need to be rented or special supplies purchased (different color filters for the various lights).
- Prior to the rehearsal, all lighting fixtures should be wired and placed as desired for the program. Setup may take some time so this team will need plenty of advanced notice.
- With lighting teams, rehearsal will be extremely important. Any dress rehearsal, or other rehearsals immediately before a production should include the lighting team. These rehearsals are opportunities for the lighting team to practice the effects that have been planned, and to take note of any special circumstances. In almost every case, rehearsal reveals new insights on how the lighting plan must be executed.
- If the lighting plan includes making adjustments to the placement of lighting fixtures during the performance, then special attention must be given to this.
- After the production, power down any equipment as necessary and permit it to cool before moving it. Put away any equipment as necessary.

EDITING AND PREPARATION OF THE RECORDINGS FOR BROADCAST OR INTERNET STREAMING

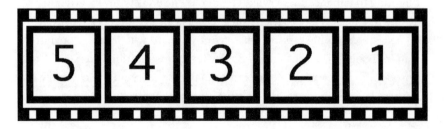

Depending on how the media team is organized, this task could be achieved by the person doing the recording, or it could be someone to whom audio or video files are provided. Regardless, duties of this person might include the following:

- Start by opening the files containing audio and/or video for the service in the software selected for editing. The files being opened should normally be in a high quality format with little or no compression.
- Add any introductory materials used in the broadcast (introductory splash audio or video, present the title screen or announce the title of the program, introductory theme music, introductory welcome to the service announcements).
- Add any exiting materials used in the broadcast (closing splash audio or video, present the farewell screen or announce the title of the program, exiting theme music, exiting farewell announcements, credits).
- Scan through the track and remove any materials that may be copyrighted and/or not permitted in the licensing for broadcast.
- Scan through the track and remove any information or presentations that may be sensitive (identifying missionaries in prohibited countries, etc.).
- Scan through the track and remove any obvious misstatements or awkward or embarrassing materials. All individuals involved in the service should be treated with respect. Humor is okay, but good judgment will help identify things that should not be broadcast.
- Identify anyone whose picture was taken during the service and confirm that permission has been granted for broadcast, or replace with a broad shot of the speaker.
- Convert any files to a format appropriate for broadcast.
- Save the program onto any necessary media required for broadcast.

OVERSIGHT OF THE CHURCH'S WEBSITE

A Website for a typical church may be maintained by a single person, or by a team of individuals. The work done to maintain the Website normally does not take place during the service like other media ministries, but this role is increasingly important. It is common for visitors to a church to have previously visited the church's Website. The Website must represent the church well, and be thoroughly professional. The Website must be modern in appearance, and contain frequently updated materials. The person maintaining the church's Website should expect to receive information regularly from the various departments in the church, but they should also expect to do substantial reporting (taking photographs and writing) on recent events. Duties of this person will include the following:

- Create a simple Web interface that permits visitors to quickly find things.
- Items such as addresses, directions, and contact information should be available on every page (click to see).
- Each ministry of the church should be described with a list of current events and photographs from recent events.
- The Web page should be registered with search engines and embedded with META tags that help bring it to the attention of those searching for it.
- Permissions to post photographs of individuals should be obtained prior to posting them.
- The churches services should be uploaded for broadcast weekly.
- The churches publications (newsletters, bulletins, etc.) should be prepared for the Web and uploaded weekly.
- The church's calendar should be published weekly.
- The Webmaster may have the responsibility for managing and maintaining e-mail accounts (pastor@mychurch.com).
- The Webmaster may have the responsibility for maintaining forms for the submission of various information (applications for special events, request for information, etc.).
- The Webmaster may have the responsibility for setting up e-commerce functions (donations to the church, etc.).
- The Webmaster may have the responsibility for the maintenance of private or protected data which is made available to the pastoral staff (membership database, etc.).

MAINTENANCE OF COMPUTER NETWORKS

The church has an increasing need for an individual who can setup and maintain computer networks, wireless networks, network disks, printers, servers, Web monitoring software, etc. The person charged with the maintenance of computer networks has some decisions that they must make which will determine the scope of their ministry:

- What services are needed (e-mail, wireless, etc.)?
- Which of these services will be locally created and maintained and which will be subcontracted or provided through an Internet portal.

The duties of this individual may include the following:

- Setup and maintain shared printers, scanners, and/or copy machines. Set church computers to use these services, or distribute information to church staff on how to use them.
- If applicable, setup and maintain any servers used by the church for the following services and oversee security and access, setting up accounts and passwords as needed.
- e-mail
- Web service
- streaming broadcast
- public or private folders
- Blogs
- Podcasts

- Install and maintain any server based applications used by the church. Many churches maintain church attendance and giving records in a database which can run on a server. Server-based applications typically allow the users to find data from a number of computers, and to permit some documents to be available to multiple users (although usually not for editing at the same time). These documents are generally password protected and only available to the users who need them. It is possible to created public folders which are not protected and care must be maintained to place only non-sensitive documents in those folders.
- Setup wired and wireless networks in a secure manner.

The media coordinator may find it useful to duplicate the lists of responsibilities found above and customize them for the specific needs of their church. These lists may be distributed to the various individuals in the ministry, or posted them near the equipment used. The media coordinator may find it especially useful to those involved in the media ministry to provide a copy of this book for each member and direct him or her to the chapter that most applies to their ministry. The chapters below explain the roles of each of these individuals in greater detail.

CHAPTER 3

Sound Reinforcement

Sound reinforcement is a necessary element of almost any contemporary church service. In the sound ministry you may be called upon to do any number of jobs, the most common being soundboard operator, and platform or stage setup, and frequently both. If you are in the main sanctuary, you may have a team to assist, but if you are operating sound for children's church, seniors, or other small group, you may be responsible for everything.

SOUNDBOARD OPERATOR, PLATFORM/STAGE SETUP

It is the responsibility of the soundboard operator to make sure the sound system is ready for use for all services to which they are assigned. This person may have responsibilities for platform and stage setup, or in a larger church, may have one or more assistants to help with setup. The soundboard operator, and any assistants, should plan to be available for any rehearsals for the service. There should be a soundcheck for musicians prior to the service. Additionally, the soundboard operator should do a soundcheck on any general purpose microphones used in the service such as those used by the speakers or choir.

Checklist of Duties:

- Setup
- Get out the appropriate microphones.
- Run and tape cables as necessary.
- Check and replace (as needed) the batteries in any devices that require them.
- Take the wireless microphone to the pastor or speaker for the day. If instruction is required for its use, teach them what to do. There are two possible strategies which may be deployed depending on the comfort of the speaker:

Strategy One—Leave the microphone on and keep the channel muted on the soundboard until the appropriate time. The obvious concern here is that the speaker is broadcasting every conversation they have, and noise around them, even if not to the house speakers. The advantage of this approach is that when it is time for the speaker, the attentive soundboard operator just turns on their channel and they are ready to go. The speaker does not have to fumble with switches or equipment. Sometimes speakers still ask if they can be heard. You may want to instruct them that this is not necessary; they just speak. You'll take care of making sure they can be heard.

Strategy Two—Turn the microphone off and teach the speaker how to turn it on before use. The clear advantage is that there is no broadcast of anything until it is time to speak. The disadvantage is that the speaker often has trouble locating the switch and turning the device on, and they still ask if they can be heard. If the speaker is familiar with the operation of the equipment, this is probably the best strategy. Otherwise, strategy one (with appropriate warnings about being broadcast) would be best.

- Turn on the soundboard (first).
- Turn on the amplifiers or powered speakers (second). Note: Shut down equipment in the opposite order.

- Un-mute and test all microphone channels on the soundboard that will be used by the worship team. Test by having an assistant speak or count into them (called a line check). It is not a good idea to tap on a microphone for a couple of reasons: (1) the resulting pops when amplified may offend anyone already in the space, (2) the resulting pops may create high level spikes which could damage equipment, depending on how the rest of the system is set. Test the input level of each microphone and adjust the preamp as needed—ideally you'll have a digital board which can remember the settings. If not, you may want to take notes, but a quick check again before the service is worthwhile. The preamp settings for permanently installed microphones should not normally change, but it's a good idea to see if they are set to their previously determined levels.
- After each instrumentalist plugs into the system, unmute their channel. Check their input level. Note, if the instrumentalists are new, show them where the inputs are. Tell them which ones to use, etc. It is especially important to check the levels of new instrumentalists and to monitor the input from their channels. The effects pedals and other equipment they use may send signals of many different strengths so there may need to be adjustments for them as they change the settings on their equipment. Watch them to see what they are doing. Any foot pedal clicks or adjustments to the volume output of their instrument may require an adjustment to the sound system.
- During rehearsal and performance, one of the greatest responsibilities of the sound tech is to balance the ensemble.
- After rehearsals and services, the sound tech should turn off any battery operated equipment.
- After rehearsals and services, the sound tech should put away any equipment that must be stored.

AN EFFECTIVE SOUNDCHECK

Most musicians are familiar enough with the setup that they know how to connect their instruments to the system. Musicians should be doing this while the sound technician is powering up the system and getting the board ready for the soundcheck. For the sound tech to be able to more easily control the main mix, each channel's input level needs to be adjusted. The best way of doing this is to have each individual instrument and vocalist play or sing just as they normally would during the service, but only one at a time. Most mixing boards have a solo function on each channel that allows you to read its level on the main LED display. While each channel receives input, adjust the trim so that the average level is 0dB, or to the level suggested by the manufacturer of the soundboard being used. Some sound techs use a standard procedure during sound check, having the drums play first, followed by the bass, guitars, keys, vocals, and others. Many studio engineers also balance instruments used in a recording in an order similar to this one.

Also, in a soundcheck, it is typical to adjust monitor levels. The sound technician might ask each individual what he or she needs to hear, but the worship leader should not hesitate to provide input on each request, if needed. (In the chapter on sound reinforcement, various monitoring techniques and strategies for obtaining a good balance in the main speakers will be given.)

Some musicians have in mind what they want but can't express it precisely. For example, it could be that a singer asks you to turn the reverb all the way up, or the treble EQ knob all the way down. In both cases, it is unlikely that this is what they truly want. A reverb unit often contains many settings and turning them all to maximum will probably give the worst possible effect. For those who are inexperienced with sound reinforcement, determining exactly what they want is more important than exactly what they say.

Still, keeping a heart that is not willfully over-reactive is important. On the flip side, musicians need to hear the same thing—when asked to change something about their performances they should do it in steps and not in extremes.

BALANCING THE ENSEMBLE

Perhaps one of the greatest responsibilities of the soundboard operator is to balance each of the musicians in the ensemble so that the sound blends as well as possible. The worship leader will be able to assist with this, and may frequently ask for a voice or instrumentalist to be louder or softer. Individual musicians may also make request for adjustments to their levels, but in order to insure that there are not too many conflicting communications coming to the soundboard operator, it is generally best to ask the musicians to direct these requests to the worship leader who will pass them along to you. Often, the worship leader does not give many instructions regarding the balance of the ensemble, so here are some tips that can be applied:

Melody: In a worship service, the melody must be easy to hear above all other parts. This is the part to which the majority of the congregation will listen and sing. It is important for them to be able to hear it to effectively worship. Generally, the worship leader will be singing the melody, but this may not always be the case. At all times, the sound tech should know who is singing the lead vocal and have their microphone prominent in the mix.

Background Vocals: Harmony parts add depth. If there are three background vocalists, ideally each would be singing a different harmony part. Try to set the balance so each can be heard in the mix. If one or more of these vocalists are singing the melody in unison with the worship leader, it is generally best to keep them softer in the mix than the others. This will avoid intonation, rhythmic, and stylistic conflicts in the melody. Rarely, a background vocalist will have a day, perhaps when they have a cold and can't hear as well, when they may sing out-of-tune. On those days, their level in the mix should be softer. Often these moments are temporary, so monitor their channel and put them back equally in the mix when possible.

Drums: In a contemporary worship service where there is no conductor, the drums help the ensemble stay together. They should be loud enough in the monitors for everyone to hear and follow. The drummer will have to work with the worship leader to establish correct tempos. Having a drummer who can keep a steady beat and follow the worship leader greatly helps the ensemble stay together.

Bass: The bass guitar plays an important role in today's worship services. Typically it plays a fundamental note on which the rest of the harmonies of the song are built. Hearing the fundamental of the chord, helps the other musicians establish the key and tune their parts. The bass may also be used to build energy and, at times to maintain the rhythmic drive of the song. Listening to recordings of the songs which are being used in worship will give the sound tech a feel for how loud or soft the bass should be in the mix.

Guitars: Typically a rhythm and a lead guitar are found in contemporary worship ensembles. The rhythm guitar is often an acoustic instrument and plays a "pad" of chords which contain rhythmic drive and harmonic definition. The lead guitar is usually an electric instrument that plays melodic notes which compliment (but don't follow) the melody of the song. The lead guitar may play the melody or improvisations upon it during instrumental interludes. The lead guitar may need more adjustments to their levels during worship than the other guitars. When they are playing a featured solo, their part should be turned up. When playing melodic fills, their instrument may not need to be as loud. If they are playing chords, then their sound should be softer still. If there are additional guitars, it is likely that some of these functions are being doubled, and the mix should not contain too much of the doubled parts. With all guitars, it is important to note that their effects pedals may send signals which vary greatly in strength. As they change their settings, it is important to make adjustments so that their place in the overall mix does not become unbalanced.

Keyboards: The piano or electronic keyboard in contemporary worship services often serve a role similar to the rhythm guitar. They play chords which provide rhythmic drive and harmonic definition. The pianist should not typically play the melody, except when it is not being sung. If the band includes both a pianist and a keyboard player, the pianist will generally fulfill this role, and the keyboard player will play long notes which add harmonic depth, but little in the way of rhythmic activity. Because the keyboard player also has a unique palette of instrumental timbres, it may also be featured at times in a role similar to the lead guitar.

Orchestral Instruments: If there is an arranger in the church, it is possible that the individuals playing orchestral parts will have materials that are very complimentary to the worship. If not, then instrumentalists will improvise parts based on their musical tastes and understanding of the style being played. The role of the orchestra may include playing "pad" sounds, providing unique timbres for instrumental solos, and providing nuanced crescendos and builds into climactic parts of the worship service.

Conflicts: It is common for instruments to serve similar roles in the worship service. For example, there could be multiple solo and/or lead instruments, multiple instruments playing rhythmic chords, etc. Normally musicians should do these in a complimentary fashion, taking turns on the lead lines, and musically supporting one another. The worship leader will typically catch and correct conflicts. Watch them carefully during the service for signals. If the worship leader does not catch problems in this area, the soundboard operator may still be able to help by adjusting the levels of the conflicting instruments so that the overall mix does not contain these problems.

Leading Instruments: Often during different parts of the worship service, different instruments take the lead in carrying the instrumental accompaniment. It is common for the guitars to provide leading harmonies and rhythms for some of the faster songs, and common for the piano or keyboards to provide this function for some of the slower songs. The soundboard operator should be attentive to which instrumentalist has the more significant role in the ensemble at times and adjust the sound reinforcement accordingly.

PLATFORM OR STAGE SETUP

There are many different stage setups possible for a modern service, but the following would be typical:

Choir Mic 1	Choir Mic 2	Choir Mic 3	Choir Mic 4
Drums	Bass Guitar		Orchestra
Keyboard and Keyboard Vocal Piano and Piano Vocal	Acoustic Guitar	Electric Guitar	And Instrumental Soloists
	Lead Vocal Podium Microphone		Background Vocals 1, 2, and 3

Because of the unique space in our church, this is the setup we use.

	Bass Guitar	Drums	Choir Mic 1	Choir Mic 2	
Piano and Vocal	Acoustic Guitar and Vocal	Electric Guitar	Lead Vocal Podium Microphone	Background Vocals 1, 2, and 3	Organ, Orchestra And Instrumental Soloists
		Kybd and Vocal			

This setup suffers from a distribution that isolates the orchestra members from the rhythm section by a good distance. Fortunately our musicians are able to make accommodations for this. For other groups, however, it might be more of a challenge.

In many churches, the instrumentalists and vocalists are spread from one side of the sanctuary to the other. The organist, if there is one, may sometimes be located in a balcony. Placing musicians in closer proximity to one another lets them communicate with one another and be attentive to the styling each plays. Since so much modern music is not completely arranged, but instead depends on the performers' abilities to improvise, placing the musicians where they can hear one another is essential.

MIKING

At any rate, the sound technician needs to know the basics of miking. We're going to start with a simple concept: Choosing the right microphone.

There are two kinds of microphones in common use in churches:

Dynamic microphones are the most common because of their dependability and ease of use. They include microphones such as the often-used Shure SM58. Their construction typically includes a wire coil which picks up sound vibrations and sends an electromagnet signal to be amplified. While every microphone should be handled with care, dynamic microphones stand up well to rough treatment. The quality of dynamic microphones may vary greatly, but by going with name-brand companies, good results are usually achieved.

Dynamic microphone

Condenser microphones are often used, especially in locations where they do not have to be moved. They are often used as choir mics. They are generally more sensitive to sound, pickup a broader frequency response than dynamic microphones, send a stronger signal to the soundboard, and have a better signal-to-noise ratio. They include microphones such as the Shure Beta 87TM. Their construction includes electronic components that require power to operate. This power typically is provided by a battery, or through the microphone cable. The power provided through a microphone cable is called phantom power. Condenser microphones are generally more delicate than dynamic microphones, and usually cost more. The issues with batteries, phantom power, and susceptibility to damage make condenser microphones a less common choice for heavy use. Their strong signals and better signal-to-noise ratio often permits their placement, especially in permanent installations.

Condenser microphone

Phantom power is an electrical current provided to the microphone from an external source such as a mixer. Most mixers have a button on each channel (or several) which permits power to be applied through the microphone lines for that channel. Phantom power is typically 48 volts DC and normally would not damage dynamic or other microphones that don't require it with the exception of older and less common ribbon microphones. Phantom power could damage equipment if connected through a bad or improperly wired cable or improperly rewired microphone or, in some cases, if run to equipment other than a microphone. Therefore, while it would not normally cause a problem, it is best to be certain that the channel receiving phantom power requires it.

Microphones—Directional Patterns

Microphones are constructed so that they pickup sound according to various patterns. Those that pickup up sound from any direction are called omni-directional. (Omni means "every," and we find it in words such as omnivore—a creature that will eat anything!) Omni-directional microphones are often used to mic large ensembles. They are better at picking up ambient sounds in a recording space, but should be placed well away from monitors or other speakers to avoid feedback.

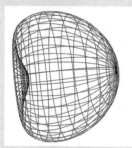

Those that pick up sounds primarily from one direction are called cardioids. (Cardioid has the same root word as cardiac and in both instances refers to the heart, or a heart-like shape.). Because they pick up sounds from one direction, Cardioid microphones tend to help eliminate feedback and are commonly used in churches. There are variations on the cardioid pattern which are referred to as hyper or super-cardioid. These typically have a tighter pickup pattern more directly in front of the microphone (a narrower and longer heart-shape). Cardioid microphones will pickup sounds outside the pickup pattern also, but those sounds are softer and more distorted.

PLACING MICROPHONES FOR VOCALS

Vocalists can generally use a hand-held microphone. Since these microphones receive heavy use, dynamic is usually the preferred choice. Because vocalists are often near monitors, a cardioid pickup pattern is preferred. Generally vocal mics are hand-held for their use, so a stand is provided more often to provide a place to put the microphone when it is not in use. Vocal microphones tend to send signals when bumped on clothing or being placed in the stands. Vocalists should be aware and use care to avoid creating extra sounds. The soundboard operator should certainly mute vocal channels when microphones are being returned to the stand. Inexperienced vocalists may hold the microphone too far away. Tell them to hold the mic about 3-inches away from their mouth. Most vocal microphones do a good job of not over accentuating pops and hisses (Consonants such as "P" and "S"). Some musicians and microphones, however, have more of an issue with this than others so it is good to keep microphone windscreens on hand if needed.

For recording vocals, it is common to use condenser microphones with a windscreen. In a studio, the mics are often placed 6-inches away.

Almost all microphones used in churches will have an XLR connector on the end. An XLR cable will plug into the microphone, and the other end of the cable will plug into a port, or snake which runs to the mixing board.

XLR connectors

PLACING MICROPHONES FOR INSTRUMENTS

Piano

The piano microphone is typically a mono microphone placed to point into the open lid of a grand or upright piano. It should generally point to the center of the strings. Checking the preamp level of this microphone is important because it is likely to be sending a strong sound. A dynamic or condenser microphone could be used for piano, but for piano, a microphone with a wide frequency response is required. The lowest A on the piano has a frequency of 27.5 hz. If the microphone picks up other nearby sound, it is okay to close the lid, exercising care to avoid placing too much strain on the cables. Stereo mics may also be used, but if so, they should be placed at a 45-degree angle to one another. Unless the piano is playing often alone, little is gained in a church setting by stereo miking.

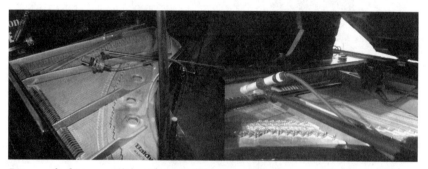

Piano miked in mono (L) and stereo (R).

Wind Instruments

Some wind instruments, depending on the size of the church and the volume of the amplified instruments, may need no sound reinforcement. This would be especially true of trumpets, and even more so when they are playing in the high register. Softer instruments such as violin and flute may need amplification. All wind instruments will need microphones if the service is being recorded for broadcast.

Most wind instruments are sufficiently loud for a good recording of a solo instrument to be obtained from as far away as three feet or more. In environments with many other instruments playing, the microphone may be placed as close as 6- to 12-inches from the instrument. With most instruments, a placement slightly lower than the instrument yields better results than overhead miking. It is always a good idea to tell a wind instrumentalist to listen to their monitor and experiment with different locations relative to the mic, and stop (or you stop them) when they find the best sound.

While standard dynamic and condenser microphones may be used for wind instruments, there are some microphones which are made specifically for wind instruments. Many of these come with clips or other mounting hardware to attach to the instrument.

Flute—Sound is strongest near the tone hole, however, the breath of the performer is also concentrated in this area. Strategies: Place the microphone near the tone hole but toward the keys to avoid too much breath.

Clarinet, Oboe, Bassoon —The sound is strongest near the bell, however, enough sound also comes from the open holes on the instrument for a good recording. Many prefer the tone near the center of the instrument. Strategy: Place the microphone near the center of the instrument, as shown to the left.

Saxophone—Sound is strongest near the bell. Many prefer to record key presses and breath noise also. Strategies: Place the microphone near the bell for a purer tone, or near the center of the instrument for tone with breath and key noises.

Trumpet, Trombone—The sound is strongest near the bell, but brass players frequently have strong articulation noises that are picked up with close miking. Strategy: Place the microphone near the bell, but not directly in front of it, typically a little lower and to one side.

Horn—The sound is strongest near the bell, but because the bell of the horn points to the back of the orchestra, frequently they have a sound wall behind them to reflect the sound toward the audience. Strategy: Place the microphone between the player and the sound wall.

Euphonium, Baritone, Tuba—These instruments typically have a bell which points up. An overhead microphone a couple of feet from the bell gives good results. Larger diaphragm microphones accentuate lower frequencies.

Percussion

For auxiliary percussion, a single mic placed a couple of feet from the instrument should pick up well. For large instruments such as marimba, there multiple microphones may be needed, or a single microphone may have to be moved to a greater distance to get even pickup throughout the range of the instrument. For marimba, not all keys will be used, so it is best to observe which area of the instrument is played and mic that area. For timpani, it would be good to mic each drum, or to use a single microphone a distance from all.

Drum Kit

For recording, a single microphone is typically placed on each tom near the head. A larger diaphragm microphone is placed near or inside the bass drum. One or two microphones may be placed on the snare (one above and one below). Sometimes a microphone may be placed to pick up both the snare and the hi-hat, but in some cases a microphone may be used specifically for the hi-hat. Usually a couple of overhead microphones are used to capture the cymbals.

In churches, it is common to place the drum set in an enclosure to that the volume of the acoustic set does not overpower other acoustic instruments. This requires miking of the drums as shown above. The drummer in such an enclosure should wear headphones with a feed from the other instrumentalists, and should wear hearing protection.

Electronic drums don't sound as natural as acoustic drums, however, they do provide an easier hookup, and potentially a benefit in spaces where the sound of acoustic drums would be louder than necessary. An electronic drum set provides a line level signal which can be run directly into a sound-board, and all instruments of the drum kit are generally already well balanced. If not, the drum set usually provides options for balancing the level of each instrument. Many people trained on acoustic drums have difficulty making the transition to electronic drums, but the benefits are (1) fewer, if any, microphones required, (2) an increased palette of sounds, (3) much easier to balance with other instruments in the worship space.

Some of the disadvantages of electronic drums include (1) a response that is not the same as acoustic drums, (2) some sounds generated by the instrument are the same, even if the instrument is struck differently, and (3) some things possible on acoustic drums, simply are not possible on electronic drums. Many special effects such as dragging a nickel over the bell of a cymbal are lost, although most drummers would be upset if you did that to their acoustic cymbals.

Acoustic Guitar

Increasingly acoustic guitars have built-in pickups, some with EQ and other effects onboard. Many acoustic guitarists run these signals into an effects box for further processing. For those circumstances where this is not the case, other options are available. A pickup may be added across the sound hole in some cases. Also, a single condenser microphone (because of the softer sound of the guitar) may be placed near the sound hole, but toward the fingerboard to avoid some of the clicking sounds created by strumming.

ELECTRONIC INSTRUMENTS

Most instruments used in church services will have a mono ¼-inch TS (tip, sleeve) jack. A ¼-inch cable will be plugged into the instrument, and the other end of the cable will be plugged into a Direct Box to convert the signal to XLR before it is run to the soundboard.

High and Low Impedance—The outputs of various audio equipment are generally high or low impedance. Most guitars, basses, and pickups for other stringed instruments have a high impedance output. The problem with high impedance outputs is that their signal degrades quickly, compared to low impedance signals. The primary function of a "direct box" is to convert a high impedance signal to a low impedance one so it can be sent over greater distances to a low impedance input on a mixing board. If the distance between a high-impedance musical instrument and the mixing board is great than 20 feet, a Direct Box should be used near the instrument and the signal should be run over a low impedance cable to the mixing board. Using the wrong cable or a cable that is too long could cause interference and result in distorted signals. Although there may be ¼-inch inputs on a 100 foot snake, they should generally not be used to carry signals from guitars and other high-impedance instruments to the mixing board.

Electric guitars including electric basses and many modern acoustic guitars have built-in pickups that send a signal similar to a microphone. Some electric guitars have electronics in them that permit them to send a line-level signal (much stronger than pickups only). Electronic keyboards send line-level signals. Some instruments, especially strings (violins, etc.), have electronic pickups installed.

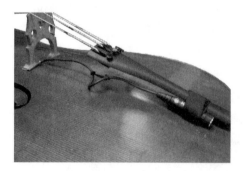

These typically send a mic-level signal. Any electronic instrument can have its signal run through a processor box (distortion and other effects for guitar, etc.).

The strength of the signal from these instruments may be line level after the processor. If a performer puts a box on bypass mode, they may be sending an instrument-level signal. If they take it off bypass, the signal may jump to line-level! This can cause a sudden and significant balance issue. Hopefully these kinds of problems will be discovered in rehearsal, but the sound technician should be aware of the possibility and ready for a quick response at all times.

A WORD ABOUT ELECTRIC GUITARS AND BASSES

Many guitarists, including bassists, prefer to play their instruments through their amplifier. In fact, some of the characteristic sounds of the instruments are only obtained by using the amplifier. Certain kinds of distortion such as natural tube distortion, certain kinds of feedback (intentional), certain EQ and other controls are only possible with the amplifier. The amplifier may contain a line out signal that can be used for some of these effects. Some effects, however, require that a microphone be used to pickup the sound of the amplifier. The guitarist can let you know when this is the case. The biggest danger of this setup is that the increased volume on the platform may compete with the existing monitors and even the house speakers. If this happens, the temptation is to raise the level of the sound in the entire sanctuary to balance the amplifiers. Instead, turning the amplifiers down so that they blend with the monitors and house speakers usually yields the best results. Most miking of amplifiers is done as shown below. Many people recommend removing the speaker grille to avoid any filtering of the sound that it may create and any noises it may make.

Microphone is placed below amp on edge of speaker.

A balanced line is one that uses special canceling technology to reduce the noise picked up by long cable runs. A balanced cable typically contains three wires: two for the signal (one positive-hot, and another negative-cold), and one wrapped around the others as a shield. The shield itself typically reduces noise. The shield is also used as a ground wire connecting the devices, which also reduces noise. Finally the two signals with opposite polarity are run through special circuitry in mixers with balanced inputs which "mix" (sum) the two signals. Any noise encountered during the travel through the cable should be removed by "cancellation." The remaining signal is the pure signal as it started at the source. Most microphones and XLR cables provide all that is needed to optimize balanced, noise canceling features if present in a mixing board.

Most electric guitars and basses use a standard mono ¼-inch cable (TS—tip, shield) also referred to as unbalanced and do not take advantage of balanced inputs. Other electronic instruments may or may not benefit from being plugged into a channel with balanced input. The instrument specifications will typically indicate if this is the case. If electronic instruments are to benefit from balanced inputs and outputs, a ¼-inch stereo cable (TRS—tip, ring, shield) must be used to connect the instrument to the mixing board. No benefit is obtained by using a balanced input, or stereo cable on an instrument which is not designed to take advantage of it. If a line is balanced, but the instrument is not, and a stereo cable is used there is no benefit or detriment to the sound. In rare cases, when running a non-balanced line into a balanced input, it may be required to insert the ¼-inch cable to the first notch. This will depend on how the device processes the balanced signal. Generally, an unbalanced line plugged into a balanced input will not produce an ill effect on the signal.

THE MIXING BOARD—HOW IT WORKS

The basic function of a mixing board is to take signals from multiple sources and electronically combine them so that they can then be amplified, processed and sent to speakers.

Of course, a glance at a modern mixing board reveals that it does much more, but this basic function is the foremost priority.

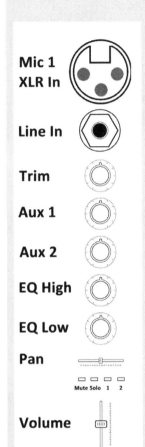

Each microphone and instrument plug into the mixing board in their own channel. Each channel goes through a series of controls (aka signal flow) depending on the mixing board. A typical channel strip with its options is shown to the left.

The first jacks at the top of the strip are the inputs. MIC 1 is an XLR input. Line In 1 is a ¼-inch input for an instrument such as a keyboard. This particular input can handle balanced (TRS) or unbalanced (TS) ¼-inch plugs.

The trim knob controls the level of the incoming signal. The purpose is to get incoming signals to the same level at this point so that they are equally processed hereafter. Most mixers have a function that lets you check the level on a visual meter of each channel after pre-amplification. Normally the signal after pre-amplification should read about zero on the mixing board's meter.

The next two options on this board are the AUX sends. The most common use of these is to send a signal to a monitor, on this board to monitor one, two, or both. More sophisticated boards have more AUX sends. It is important to note how the board routes the aux sends. Some do so before the EQ while others allow the user to modify the routing to be either pre or post the EQ. Aux sends can also be either Pre or Post fader. Pre, which is used for monitor sends, indicates that the level sent to the monitors will not be affected by the fader adjustments on that channel. Instrumentalists and vocalists hear in their monitor the signal that they are sending into the board, and not the signal as it will eventually sound in the house speakers. AUX Sends don't have to be directed to a monitor. The output of an AUX send can be sent to an effects processor instead. If so, then another channel (or two) on the board would commonly be used as an input for the effects processor, so the reverb or other effects can be heard.

The next three knobs on this board are for EQ (equalization). This permits the sound to be modified so that there are more or less treble, middle, or bass frequencies.

The next knob is the pan knob and determines how much of this signal is directed to the left speaker and how much to the right speaker.

The next two buttons are the mute and solo buttons.

The final control is the gain, often called the volume fader, and controls the amount of this channel that is directed to the house speakers. On most boards, this is a sliding control, rather than a rotary one as shown.

ABOUT INPUT SIGNALS

Every device that is plugged into a mixing board provides different signal strength. That is why pre-amplification is necessary in a mixing board—to adjust all incoming signals to an equivalent level for the remaining processing that will occur in the board. There are three common levels of signals that enter a board:

Mic-level—This is the softest signal of the three usually in the -40dB to -60dB range .

Instrument-level—This would be a level close to the mic level and is the level typically sent by guitar pickups. This level is sometimes referred to as consumer level and is -10dB.

Line-level—This is generally referring to a balanced output and is the level that would be sent by an electronic keyboard, some guitar effects processors, or a similar device. Line level is +4dB.

The mixing board has main out lines which are directed to amplifiers then to the house speakers. It also has AUX out lines, which are typically sent to amplifiers then to the monitors. On many mixing boards, it is possible in the channel strip to assign each channel to one of several sub-master groups. Usually a switch on the channel lets you specify if the sound should be routed to sub 1, 2, 3, or 4 (etc.). These sub assignments can be defined by the pan knob. Left sends to the odd channel and right sends to the even while a pan knob set at twelve o'clock is sent to both odd and even busses. All channels assigned to a sub may then be controlled by a separate volume slider. This may make balancing the performing ensemble easier because instead of adjusting several sliders for the guitars, or several sliders for the vocalists, all may be turned up or down by moving the volume slider for that sub.

WIRELESS MICROPHONE SYSTEMS

Wireless microphone systems work as follows. Each wireless microphone includes a transmitter that runs on a battery installed in the microphone. Each transmitter has an accompanying receiver. Typically, the receiver is located near the mixing board and a signal from the receiver runs into an input on the mixing board. Each wireless microphone requires its own receiver and channel on the mixing board. If the mixing board is too far away from the wireless microphone to receive the signal, the receiver may have to be placed so that its output is routed to a snake that goes to the designated channel in the mixing board.

Wireless microphones come in three common forms, a lapel microphone used primarily for presenters, an over-the-ear microphone and a handheld used primarily for musical vocals. Each wireless microphone set used should receive and transmit on different frequencies. It is common for these devices to contain switches that permit the easy selection of non-conflicting channels. Normally this is only a concern during the initial setup of the equipment. See the manual that came with the equipment for details. A helpful online resource indicating which frequencies work best in the various areas of the United States is found at http://www.shure.com.

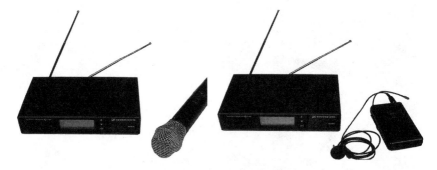

IN-EAR MONITORING SYSTEMS

There are a number of in-ear monitoring systems including some that use wireless technology. In one Sennheiser system, a signal from the mixing board (from an AUX send) is sent to a wireless transmitter. Musicians wear a receiver with headphones or ear buds to listen to the monitor mix. As many receivers as desired can tune into the transmitter. In this system, all musicians hear the same monitor mix. If multiple mixes are required, additional transmitters each with corresponding receivers can be purchased.

In another system by Aviom, the signal of every instrument is is routed into a box which digitizes it using Aviom's proprietary format A- Net®, and sends over CAT 5 cables to units that provide a custom mix for each musician. Usually independent controllers are run to the drummer, the bass player, the guitarists, the keyboard players, and the background and/or lead vocals. Normally these mixes are run to headphones, but those for vocals are commonly run to an amplifier then to a monitor, because of the need for many people to share the mix.

Aviom Setup

AVIOM SETUP—Inputs from the mixing board are routed into the Aviom Input Module. The input module digitizes the sound and sends the encoded signal over an Ethernet Cat 5 cable to a routing box which distributes the compressed sounds to as many personal Aviom mixing devices as needed (the limit is usually 16 or 64, depending on the equipment purchased). Each person who has an Aviom mixer can create a custom mix which can be sent to an amplifier or to headphones or earbuds.

In-ear monitoring systems provide a significant advantage in that the sound level on the platform can be greatly reduced. Monitors used on stage sometimes are loud enough to interfere with the house mix. The biggest disadvantage is frequently the difficulty of hearing acoustic instruments, the congregation singing, the acoustics of the performance space, and spoken instructions that do not occur into a microphone. All of these problems can be solved with additional miking, or by using headphones that permit the sound of the performance space to be heard with the mix. Those using an Aviom system frequently use earbuds. While the quality of sound is usually good, earbuds typically filter out more of the surrounding sound than headphones.

A WORD ABOUT MONITORING

Monitors are often necessary for a person to hear the other members of the ensemble so they can stay together. Monitors are also used to amplify the sound of an individual performer's part, so they can hear themselves and play better. In a loud performance space, this is often necessary. In a perfect world, every performer would be making a significant musical contribution to the ensemble, and no mix other than the house mix would be needed because each performer could hear themselves in the mix. This, of course, puts a lot of responsibility on the performers and the soundperson—all must be functioning nearly perfectly. In most cases, the house mix may fade some performers so far back in the mix they can't hear themselves, and this would be especially problematic for instrumentalists who rely heavily on their ears for tuning or playing in the right key. It is especially easy for a guitarist to get one fret off when playing their scale patterns if they can't hear themselves. It is also difficult for fretless players (violin, viola, cello, string bass, fretless electric bass, even trombone) to tune if they can't hear themselves.

The two biggest problems with monitoring are as follows:

- The sound from the monitors is so loud it interferes with the house mix.
- The monitors do not provide performers with information they need to play or sing to their best level.

Many monitors are placed on the floor so that they can be heard by a large number of individuals (choir members, orchestra, etc.). Some monitors, especially during worship and/ or concerts are directed toward one individual (the guitarist, bassists, drummer, etc.), or a few individuals. In these cases, it makes sense to raise the monitors so they are closer to these individuals. It takes much less energy for a monitor that is closer to the performer than one which is farther away. Consequently, there is much less sound from the monitors that would interfere with the house mix.

MEDIA PLAYERS

Any number of media players will be required. A few that may be needed are listed below:

Computer—frequently used to play CDs and DVDs. Can be used to play media from the Internet. Can be used to play other video files (.mov—Quicktime, wmv—Windows Media Video, .flv—Flash Video, etc.). Can be used to play other audio formats (.mp3, .aac, .wav, .aif, etc.). Sound is run through the soundboard. Video is run through the projector. The computer should be equipped with as many inputs as possible (USB Key Disk, CD, DVD, Firewire—for external hard drives, or direct video, camera card reader, etc.)

CD Player—frequently done using the CD drive of a computer, but sometimes a separate CD player is used.

DVD Player—the sound will run through the board. The video through the projector—frequently done using the DVD drive of a computer, but sometimes a separate DVD player is used. If a separate DVD player is used, the projector may have to be switched to a different input (usually difficult to accomplish within a service) or a switch box may be required to select either the computer or DVD as the source.

There are some media players that you are not likely to need because they have become obsolete as of this writing: cassette tape player, phonograph, 8-track tape player, reel-to-reel tape player. Still, you may want to keep a list of people you know who have one of these, just in case it is needed.

DECIBEL METER

One of the biggest complaints a sound person is likely to receive is that the music is too loud. A decibel meter is a measuring device that lets you determine exactly how loud the music is in a certain spot. It is a good idea to monitor the volume of the music in the service to make sure it is within the range that you desire. The perfect level (how loud is just right) is a subjective one. Some congregations will want an environment like a rock concert where the levels may peak at 95dB (or louder). Most, however, will prefer peaks around 80 to 85dB. If a meter will be used often to set the levels within the sanctuary, it is a good idea to have several decision makers on hand and gradually turn the system up until the consensus is that the sound is just right for worship. That level would then become the maximum. It is important to note that this level is established by the human ear. The decibel meter, then becomes a means of helping insure that level is respected in future worship services. When monitoring the volume level, it is important to take measures from various locations in the sanctuary. It is always a good idea to know where the louder and softer spots in the sanctuary are so you can direct people to a location which better suites their taste.

Decibel meters can also be used to measure the level of monitors on the platform and sound in the sanctuary. Decibel meters may provide concrete information supporting the need for changes in overall volume.

A question might arise about how soft is too soft in worship. Well, of course the music must always be heard, so 60dB or so might be a good minimum level, but it is unlikely that the music will ever reach that low a point. Even so, silence (near 0db) is also effective in worship at times, so a reasonable minimum is 0dB.

dB Chart

0—softest audible sound

60—normal conversation

90 to 100dB—lawn mower—hearing damage with long or repeated exposures

120 to 140dB—jet engine at close range—hearing damage with short exposure

TESTING EQUIPMENT

Pink noise generators create all frequencies commonly used in music and can be played in a space to balance the equalization (EQ) of the system. A calibrated microphone is placed to pickup the pink noise and all frequencies are then adjusted using controls on the EQ units in the system. Ideally, all frequencies should be amplified in the same proportions by the sound-reinforcement equipment. Using this gear, a sound system can be adjusted to take into account any frequency amplification that may occur in the equipment, or in the acoustics of the environment. A hand-held oscilloscope is sometimes used to test for the presence of audio signals and to determine their characteristics. There are a variety of cable testers that will check the connections in standard audio cables. These are particularly useful when repairing cables. Some testing equipment combines several devices into one unit. For example, Phonic makes a device that contains a decibel meter, pink noise generator, and oscilloscope.

ACOUSTICALLY TREATING A SANCTUARY

Acoustics is an imprecise art that is often practiced after a building is completed rather than before. If a space has large, hard, and flat surfaces, especially those that are parallel, it is possible that sound could travel through the space in a manner that will create muddy or unclear sounds, particularly in music.

Almost anyone who has performed music in a typical high school gymnasium understands the problems that can be created. Fortunately most worship spaces don't have that many problems, but some do. The biggest symptom indicating that there are acoustic problems are complaints from the congregation. If several members mention how difficult it is to understand the speaker, or how "awful" the music is, it's probably a good idea to consider an acoustic treatment.

There are formulas that let you calculate how "live" an acoustic space is based on the square footage of hard walls, carpet, and other materials found in the sanctuary. These formulas typically yield a value which can be compared to a chart to indicate if it falls within the acceptable acoustic range for the intended use. One such system is described here: http://www.aes.org/e-lib/browse.cfm?elib=1462.

A great number of acoustic adjustments, however, can be made by simply experimenting within the space. If the space is too live (too many parallel, hard, flat walls with much echo), it is possible to hang curtains or other fabrics that reduce the echo. In the rare event that a room is too dead (all walls are draped, all floors are carpeted, the ceiling has sound absorbing panels), it is possible to increase the reverberation of the room by strategically mounting hard flat panels, or sound dispersion panels, etc.

AMPLIFIERS

Just how many amplifiers are needed in an acoustic space is a question that frequently arises in sound setup. The following will serve as a general guide:

- One for the house speakers (or for each set of house speakers).
- One for each monitor.

Operating a stereo system requires approximately twice as many amplifiers for each stereo pair of speakers.

It is also important to match amplifiers and speakers according to their resistance ratings. An amplifier may be rated to supply 4 ohm or 8 ohm speakers. Mismatching speakers and amplifiers could result in the shortened life of either device.

COMMON PROBLEMS—PREVENTION AND SOLUTIONS

Prevention: Communicating During the Service

The musicians on stage will often need adjustments to their monitors during the service. A system of hand signs is usually developed to facilitate this communication. Here are some suggestions for hand signs:

- Turn something up—thumbs up
- Turn something down—thumbs down (don't be obvious lest the congregation think you disapprove).
- How will you know what to turn up? Person giving signals will point to the monitor, speaker, or instrument needing to be adjusted then give the up or down signal.
- Keys up—wiggle fingers as though playing keys, then turn-up signal.
- Guitar up—strum air guitar, then turn-up signal.
- Turn my microphone up in the mix—tap pointer finger on the microphone.
- When a successful adjustment has been made, give the okay sign so the sound person knows everything is okay.

Communication via hand signs during a service is fraught with difficulties. For example, often a signal to turn an instrument down is received by the sound man, but then that instruments starts playing more softly before any adjustment can be made. The person sending the signal may give the okay before any adjustment is made. If the "okay" signal is missed, the soundboard operator may still turn the signal down, and then the two may engage in a longer set of signals which ultimately end up with settings close to where they started. Enjoy these moments!

Solutions: Microphone is Silent

A silent microphone requires that the signal path be traced from the microphone to the amplifier. At some point a problem will be discovered. First, check the following *on the board* because (1) it's assumed that the items below would normally have been taken care of already, and (2) while at the board, you can be dealing with other sound issues as needed.

- Is the system on and amplifying other incoming instruments correctly?
- Is the microphone muted on the board
- Is the volume fader turned up enough?
- Is level appearing on the meter for that channel?
- Is the preamplification in the mixing board turned up enough?

Physical Connections

If it has a switch, is the microphone turned on? If there is a microphone switch, it is recommended that they be taped in the on position and that the sound person turn the microphone on and off by muting the channel when needed. A switch is simply another opportunity for performers to accidentally sabotage their own performance.

- If a condenser microphone has a battery, is it known to be good?
- If the microphone requires phantom power, is it on?
- Is the microphone plugged into a cable running to the system?
- Are all the cables running to the system plugged in?
- Are all of the cables good? Try different cables. If a bad cable is discovered, replace it with a good one and place the bad one in the bin to be repaired or replaced.
- Is there a bad channel on the snake (try plugging in another channel)? If a bad channel is discovered, mark it as bad with tape on both ends and report it to the media coordinator.
- If the microphone is wireless, is the battery fresh (always keep fresh batteries on hand)?

- Is the microphone/transmitter on?
- Is the receiver on?
- Is the receiver wired correctly into the soundboard with working cables?

MICROPHONE CRACKLES, CLICKS, OR STATIC

- Check the cable going to the microphone. That is the most common reason for crackling, especially if the sound occurs when a cable is moved. Cables with a lifetime warranty are inexpensive and are usually easily obtained locally. When a cable goes bad, trade it in (or toss it and buy another, or repair it).
- If there are other wires going to the system from the microphone, check them also.
- Check any points of connection. Connectors are another weak point in the signal path. It is easy for floor connectors to be stepped on or kicked with damage resulting. Replacing the jacks may be necessary. Strategy: Try plugging into different ports.

TESTING A CABLE

Inexpensive testing equipment is available from your local music store or audio/video center. Plug both ends of a microphone cable into the test equipment—lights will indicate good and bad connections. It is a good idea to move the cable, especially near the connectors so that any loose connections can be detected at that time.

WIRING AND RESOLDERING A CABLE

The equipment needed for wiring and resoldering a cable are a soldering iron, rosin core electrical solder (thin gauge), a soldering tool (for manipulating wires when they're too hot), and a clamp (for holding the items to be soldered).

Instructions

- Turn on the soldering iron and permit it to heat to temperature.
- Once hot, if necessary, clean the tip of the iron so that there are no debris remaining. This can be accomplished with a damp sponge.
- Melt a little solder on the tip of the iron to make certain it is hot enough.
- Connect the wire to the location to be soldered with a good physical connection. Typically the wires should be twisted so that they would hold or work even without solder. Make certain the wires are touching only the contacts or wires that they should be touching and no others.
- Because in the next operation you will be holding a soldering iron in one hand, and solder in the other, you may need to place the wires to be soldered into a clamp to keep them from moving during soldering.
- Touch the tip of the soldering iron to the underside of the wires to be soldered and permit them to heat to a temperature that will melt the solder.
- Touch the solder to the top of the wires to be soldered and let the solder melt into the wires toward the soldering iron. Do not apply too little or too much solder.
- If necessary, use the soldering tool to adjust the wires while they are hot.

- When the solder has covered the wires and/or contacts, remove the iron and solder and give the connection time to cool.
- Once the solder is completely cool, examine the joint to make certain that it is snug. There should be a complete bonding of the two wires being soldered. There should be no wires touching the soldered joint except those that should be. There should be no droplets of solder that have fallen into the other parts of the wiring.

There should be no melting of the insulation around the wire that leaves bare wire exposed.

The diagram below shows how to wire and solder ¼-inch mono (TS) jacks. Note the wiring colors may differ but the connection to the tip and sleeve of the jack should be as shown, and should be the same on both ends of the cable. Once soldered, a cable tester as shown below may be used to determine if the cable is working properly.

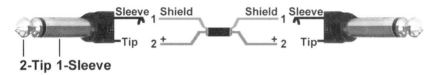

2-Tip 1-Sleeve

¼-inch Stereo

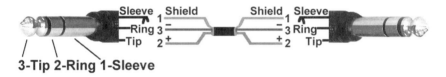

3-Tip 2-Ring 1-Sleeve

XLR

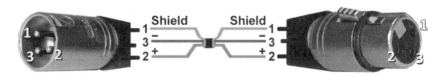

Cable Tester

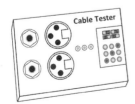

THERE IS A HUM IN THE MONITORS OR HOUSE SOUND

Here are a few troubleshooting tips to try if there is a hum in the monitors or house sound:

- During soundcheck, first mute each channel one at a time. If the hum disappears when one on of the channels is muted, the hum is coming either from the instrument, cables plugged into that channel, effects boxes used by that instrument, a direct box used by that instrument, or something in the board or signal path of that channel.
- Try putting the instrument into another channel. If the hum disappears then reappears, it is most likely the instrument, a cable, direct box, or effects box. Try replacing each until the problem is solved. Players are sometimes resistant to the idea that there may be a problem with their instrument, but if possible, they should have a professional check their instrument. Just because their instrument works fine with their amplifier doesn't mean it is in perfect working order. Some problems with instruments simply do not show up with some amplifiers. If the hum does disappear when the instrument is plugged into another channel, the instrument is eliminated as a possible source of the hum. The hum could still be the cables leading from the instrument to the previous channel of the soundboard, or something in the board or signal path of the previous channel. If the instrument is eliminated as a source of hum, troubleshooting should continue with the previous channel when time permits.
- If the hum does not disappear when all channels are muted, try dragging the main faders up or down. If the hum remains the same, the hum is probably in the amplifiers or connections to the speakers. One thing to try is turning the amplifiers down, and turning the soundboard up. This will occasionally reduce or eliminate amplifier hum.
- If the hum gets louder or softer as the main faders are adjusted up or down (and all instruments have been muted), the hum is probably originating in the soundboard. It's still worthwhile to work with the board as much as possible to see if any AUX sends or returns

are the source of the problem, or if the hum can be isolated on the soundboard (for example, it only occurs when on-board compression or reverb are used). In most cases, the soundboard will have to go in for service when this happens.

FEEDBACK

There are two levels of feedback with which you will frequently deal:

Level One feedback is mild and you notice that it comes in and out as the music gets louder or softer. It is a light and occasional ringing. Except in rare circumstances, feedback always involves a microphone (note—a guitar pickup is also a type of microphone—but your first suspect is always a regular microphone). The on-stage monitors and house speakers are also sometimes contributing factors in creating feedback. If there are many open microphones in the system, mute them one at a time until the culprit is discovered. Turn each back on if it is okay. Once the offending microphone is discovered, either move it (or the person holding it) further from the speakers, or turn down the gain on that microphone. If it turns out a guitar pickup is the source of the feedback, move it further from the amplifier. A guitar pickup usually needs to be close to a loud monitor to generate feedback.

Level Two feedback is offensive to the point that everyone in the space is grabbing their ears. Immediately pull down the main faders. If all microphones are grouped on the board as vocals, pull down the vocals instead. If that doesn't solve the problem, pull down the main faders. If possible, turn the faders slowly back up until a light ringing feedback appears. Solve it as you would level-one feedback. Some boards have lights that help you quickly identify the source of feedback. In almost all cases, the overload light of a channel producing feedback will be lit steady. If you have a quick eye, check all microphone channels and mute or adjust the ones with the steady overload light. When placing inputs in the soundboard, it's a good idea to group vocal mics together on consecutive channels for circumstances like this.

SOUND IS METALLIC

This is generally indicative of a channel that has treble EQ turned to high, and one in which there is possibly some feedback. Turn down the treble and turn up the middle and bass frequencies as needed. Also examine the position of the microphone in relation to speakers and see if any adjustments need to be made.

SOUND IS BOOMING

This is generally indicative of a channel that has bass EQ turned to high. Turn down the bass and turn up the treble and mid frequencies as needed.

SOUNDTRACK WON'T PLAY

The soundtrack for a soloist is usually played by a device (CD player, DVD player, computer, tape player, etc) that is not used as often as the others on the soundboard. Follow the signal path from the sound source to the soundboard. In the case of a computer, there are sometimes software and hardware settings that control the volume or signal. It is important to check each of those.

If a signal is arriving at the soundboard, make certain the channels are unmuted, preamplification is set appropriately, the gain and master gain are turned up, and the system is working properly. If the signal is not coming into the soundboard, troubleshoot the signal path from the source to the soundboard. Check to see if the cables from the device to the soundboard are properly in place.

MUSICIANS NOT STAYING TOGETHER, CAN'T HEAR EACH OTHER, CAN'T HEAR THEMSELVES, OR ARE OUT OF TUNE

You can usually tell that monitoring is not optimum when the musicians have trouble playing together, or individual musicians start playing wrong notes or singing out of tune, or they start playing or singing too loudly. The reasons a monitor may be incorrectly set are numerous. Possibly the logical settings on the board just don't produce a good mix. Possibly one musician asked to hear so much of their instrument, the others cannot hear themselves. It is important to have a good balance of all instruments in most monitors, with slight adjustments for the persons playing near those monitors (so they can hear if they are singing in tune, playing the right notes, etc.) Ideally, the house mix will be perfect, every instrument will be making a musical contribution and can be heard. Ideally, the house mix is all that should be provided to the monitors. In reality, however, this is seldom achieved. The best thing is to set the monitors so that the musicians can hear what they need. Typically they can tell you what they need, but sometimes, their requests create problems. During the rehearsal, the worship leader and soundman should walk to each monitor and listen to see if an appropriate mix is found there.

There is a commonly circulated idea that some songs are piano driven or guitar driven. In truth, all songs are performed by a worship team who must think and play together as one. Because there is frequently no conductor, the ensemble depends on the rhythm section (piano, bass, guitar), but these must follow the worship leader (right or wrong). It is the worship leader's responsibility to keep the team together and to make certain they do not fall into the trap of prideful thinking.

SPEAKER MIC HAS REVERB, SOLOIST DOES NOT

The easiest way to troubleshoot this issue may be to have the speaker and worship leader trade microphones, however, this may not always be possible or desirable. Troubleshooting this issue may depend on how the reverb is configured on the specific sound system. The solution will be similar, but the most likely possibilities are as follows:

- An AUX Send is used to provide a signal from any channels needing reverb to an external reverb unit. An AUX Return or separate Mixer Channel is receiving those channels with reverb or any effects applied. To correct this, turn the Aux Send which directs sound from

the speaker's microphone to the reverb unit all the way down, and
turn the AUX Send on the soloist's microphone up appropriately.

- An AUX Send or Effects Send is providing a signal from any
  channels needing reverb to an internal reverb unit. Depending on
  the board used, the output from the unit may be mixed directly into
  the output or directed to a sub section of the mixing board where
  it can be determined how much of the processed sound should be
  included in the final mix. The solution is more or less the same. Find
  the Aux Send or Effects Send control for the speaker channel and
  turn it down all the way. Find the control for the soloists channel
  and turn it up appropriately.

CHAPTER 4

Projection

PROJECTION

For every worship service, there should be a separate person in charge of projection. Duties of this position were described in Chapter 1 and are amplified below. The projection ministry may involve a number of volunteers:

Projection Operator: This person operates the projection equipment during services. They keep the lyrics in sync with the worship. They show announcements, sermon notes, Bible verses, etc.

Data Entry: There may be one or more persons who prepare the materials for projection. Those materials may include songs, notes, outlines, Bible verses, and more.

Graphic or Presentation Designer: This person is responsible for creating unique graphics for the service which are used in projected presentations.

Camera Operators: If there will be live video projected, camera operators will be required.

Video Producer: If multiple cameras are used, a video producer will be actively involved in video selection, mixing and effects.

One of the big questions for the projection ministry is, "What is to be projected?" Most smaller churches project announcements, lyrics, and sermon notes. Larger churches may project video of the speaker, soloists, orchestra, and more.

LYRICS AND SERMON NOTES

There are a number of projection software programs available for displaying lyrics and other items used in the worship service. It is common to use PowerPoint to show announcements and sermon notes (because the pastor or his secretary may have prepared them using PowerPoint). It is also common to use dedicated software for the projection of lyrics.

DESIGN PRINCIPLES

When putting items on the screen for display, it is best to limit the text to just a few lines (usually no more than six). Under some circumstances eight lines may be used, but if that is the case, it is best to chunk the lines together in groups of four.

Heavenly Father, Spirit, Son

God of all the ages

Help me to hear Your still, small voice

God of all the ages

GOD OF ALL THE AGES, ©2008, FLOYD RICHMOND

Endless, boundless, mighty God

God of all the ages,

Pure and holy, perfect God,

God of all the ages

GOD OF ALL THE AGES, ©2008, FLOYD RICHMOND

Heavenly Father,

Spirit, Son

God of all the ages,

Help me to hear

Your still small voice

God of all the ages.

GOD OF ALL THE AGES, ©2008, FLOYD RICHMOND

Endless, boundless,

Mighty God

God of all the ages,

Pure and holy,

Perfect God,

God of all the ages.

GOD OF ALL THE AGES, ©2008, FLOYD RICHMOND

Heavenly Father, Spirit, Son
God of all the ages
Help me to hear Your still small voice
God of all the ages
Endless, boundless, mighty God
God of all the ages,
Pure and holy, perfect God,
God of all the ages

GOD OF ALL THE AGES, ©2008, FLOYD RICHMOND

Heavenly Father, Spirit, Son
God of all the ages
Help me to hear Your still small voice
God of all the ages

Endless, boundless, mighty God
God of all the ages,
Pure and holy, perfect God,
God of all the ages

GOD OF ALL THE AGES, ©2008, FLOYD RICHMOND

If the slides will be broadcast to traditional television, text should not be placed near the edge of the screen.

When choosing background images, choose images that are generic or that support the theme of the song. For example, songs about God's majesty should have generic backgrounds or pictures reflecting His majesty.

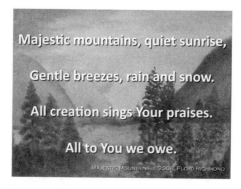

When choosing colors for text and background, make certain there is high contrast. Avoid, for example, using dark text of any color on a dark background.

HEAVENLY FATHER, SPIRIT, SON
GOD OF ALL THE AGES
HELP ME TO HEAR YOUR STILL SMALL VOICE
GOD OF ALL THE AGES
ENDLESS, BOUNDLESS, MIGHTY GOD
GOD OF ALL THE AGES,
PURE AND HOLY, PERFECT GOD,
GOD OF ALL THE AGES

HEAVENLY FATHER, SPIRIT, SON
GOD OF ALL THE AGES
HELP ME TO HEAR YOUR STILL SMALL VOICE
GOD OF ALL THE AGES

ENDLESS, BOUNDLESS, MIGHTY GOD
GOD OF ALL THE AGES,
PURE AND HOLY, PERFECT GOD,
GOD OF ALL THE AGES

Compare the contrast of these six slides with the ones on page 71.

OPERATIONAL PRINCIPLES

During rehearsal, check the display of the text against the background. Projectors vary in the brightness of their bulb and what looks great on the computer screen may not look as good when projected. Make any adjustments necessary.

The software may take a brief moment to display the material after the operator moves to the next screen. The operator must give the signals a few seconds early so the lyrics are ready for the next section of the song in time. Some worship leaders make this process easy by rehearsing a song and consistently doing it the same way. Other worship leaders are likely to rearrange the song during the worship. If the worship leader is of the latter type, it is likely that hand signals have been worked out with the members of the band so they can follow him or her. Commonly used hand signs are found below.

  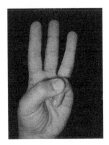

One Finger = Verse 1, Two Fingers = Verse 2, Three Fingers = Verse 3 or Pre Chorus

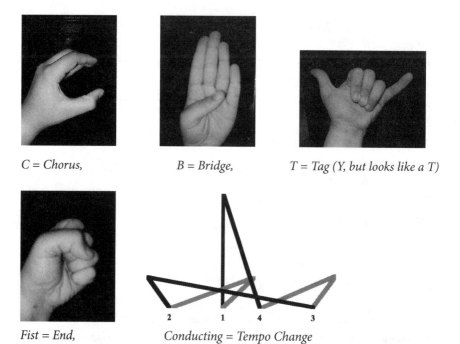

C = Chorus,   B = Bridge,   T = Tag (Y, but looks like a T)

Fist = End,   Conducting = Tempo Change

Although these terms are related to those you might find in classical music, not all (especially bridge) are used the way a classical musician would typically use them. For example:

- Verse 1, and verse 2 typically tell the story of the song.
- The prechorus, if it exists, typically builds the intensity and often uses the same lyrics for every verse.
- The chorus is typically the most intense part of the song and is the place where the theme of the song is most emphasized.
- A bridge is simply a contrasting section, either soft or loud, that may be used to focus the worshiper on a different aspect of the message of the song. Some songs without bridges have an instrumental with free worship inserted at this point.
- The chorus immediately after the bridge is often sung differently than the other choruses (frequently with voices and drums only, or perhaps with a different instrumental accompaniment).

- The last chorus, is usually fully developed with all instruments playing with full energy.

While the worship leader's intention is to give many of these signals discretely (so the congregation does not see or become distracted), it is wise to be as observant as possible so you can anticipate where the song is going to go. Even if you can not see the signals, it is often possible to anticipate where the song is going by the performances of the musicians who can see the signals. For example, it is common for the music to build differently at the end of the bridge when the intention is to return to the chorus, than when the worship leader intends to go elsewhere.

If there is no other indication of how the song is going to unfold, a common assumption is as follows: Intro, V1, C, V2, C, (C), B, (B), C, (C), Tag.

There are many variations on this scheme. Some songs have multiple bridges, and/or instrumentals. Some songs have additional verses. Some songs insert quotes from familiar hymns. It would be impossible to indicate them all, but the form above is common and should give you an idea of what's going to happen.

CHECKLIST

Before the Rehearsal

- Secure the list of songs for the service and enter or download them into the projection software. Many of the software programs permit you to download these directly from services such as CCLI. All will let you copy and paste lyrics onto a screen at a time. Some will let you paste the entire lyrics into the program then format them, or choose which ones you want to use on each screen. Others require you to paste them into your software a screen at a time.
- Get copies of any DVDs, computer videos, announcements, or promotional PowerPoints or other media to be displayed and prepare them for presentation. The projection software and the DVDs or computer movies are often played through different systems. Still, the projectionist will be responsible for all of them. This means that they

will need to rehearse switching from the projection software to the DVD player so that when the time comes, they are able to do so with ease. It is also critical that they rehearse with any DVDs that are to be used. DVDs can be created with any number of different methods of operation. Some start playing immediately upon being inserted. With others, there are menus and submenus which must be used. With one recent DVD encountered by the author, the screen action stopped before the movie started and a small red button flashed in the lower left corner. There were no instructions on the screen, but this red button had to be clicked to continue. The projectionist must attend practice to identify these issues in advance. Also, various computers and DVD players work in different manners. When computers are used to play DVDs, a number of special problems may occur. The operator should know how to switch into full screen mode, rather than showing the video in a small window. In the case of computers with multiple video cards (one for control and anther for presentation), it will be necessary to know how to place the DVD onto the screen being projected.

- Get copies of sermon notes and/or outlines, Bible verses, or other information to be displayed and enter them into the projection software. The temptation with sermon notes, especially when prepared by those without presentation experience is to place too much information on a screen, or to use fonts that are too small. A good rule of thumb is to use no more than four to six lines of text on a screen. If as many as eight must be used, it is again wise to chunk the content into different sections so that the eye can easily follow the organized information.

- Place screens, turn on projectors, etc. In most worship services, the projectors are permanently mounted to the ceiling or walls. This requires that they be turned on with remotes. In large worship services, it is common to use multiple projectors, perhaps one on the left and one on the right. It is not uncommon to project to a back wall also for the worship team and members of the stage. Normally all of these projectors receive the same signal, but the setup of these projectors should be so that the signals sent to each can be selected from the projectionist booth. The projector on the back wall, could for example, be used independently to project prompts for a drama. At any rate, each of these projectors that is mounted out of reach will need to be turned on with a remote. Fresh batteries for the remote must be kept onhand also, because turning some of the projectors on manually would be difficult. Any screens that are retractable or not in place for worship must be placed as needed. Usually a switch raises or lowers a retractable screen.

- If video from a live feed will be projected, there should be one or more camera operators and perhaps a video production team providing that signal. Check to make certain the signal for the live feed is active. Some large churches, or worship events in large spaces, project video of the service to screens around the auditorium. If that is your responsibility, coordinate with this team to make certain you have a signal to project.

At Rehearsal

- Run through the entire service making notes about anything out of the ordinary. Again, regular services become routine, but special services require greater preparation. Usually an order of service is prepared by the pastor and/or his staff and distributed to those who need it. The media coordinator may look over the list, add notes, and distribute it to the media team. This should have any order of service should indicate when any DVDs or other media items are to be presented. Often, items used in the sermon, or in announcements are not rehearsed, so it is necessary for the projectionist to run through them to make certain that everything works as expected. Often, a rehearsal reveals special problems (for example, the worship leader wants to sing a chorus from an earlier song at the end of the worship set).
- Power down and put away any equipment as needed after the service. Projectors in particular should be off as often as possible. This preserves their bulb's life. It is also important that projectors are

turned off using their remote, rather than by switching off a power switch. Commonly after a projector is shut down, it goes through a cooling phase which is important for the life of the equipment.

The Service

- Place screens, turn on projectors, etc. This will be similar to what was done in preparation for rehearsal.
- Double check to see that everything is ready. Any media used (DVDs, computer files, etc.) should be where they are needed.
- Double check the "order of service" to make certain nothing has changed. While this will be rare, sometimes circumstances dictate that there are changes which could impact the projectionist. Check with the media coordinator or pastors to make certain there have been no changes.
- Attentively execute the plans as rehearsed. Having said that, it is important to expect the unexpected. There will be times when you must think on your feet.
- Afterward, power down and put away equipment as needed. This will be similar to what was done in rehearsal.
- File (or delete) any records of the service as needed. Some churches will keep records of sermon notes, lyrics projected, etc. Others will delete the old files. Find out what the expectation is and do any necessary clean-up as required. Return DVDs, USB drives, or other media to any guests who brought them.

PROJECTING VIDEO OF THE SERVICE

In large churches or spaces, it may be difficult for the audience to see the facial expressions or gestures of the pastor, worship leaders, and musicians because of the distance. The service is often more effective if video can be projected (often referred to as IMAG). In some cases, the speaker may be so small in the eyes of the congregation, that it is preferable for those in attendance to watch the video. If the services are being recorded for broadcast or Internet streaming, it is often possible to get a video feed from this source. Normally the output from a video camera will be directed to the projectionist's booth and at the appropriate times, the projectionist will select this camera signal for display. In Christian Music Concerts, it may be appropriate to have multiple projections happening at the same time (the lead vocalist may be projected to one screen, and the other musicians to other screens). In a worship service, having the worship team and lyrics projected to different screens may be appropriate. To get started with the projection of speakers requires the addition of cameras, and possibly video mixing equipment. This is discussed in more detail in the recording video chapter. The projectionist ministry, however, may involve a projectionist, one or more camera operators, and sometimes an individual running a video mixing board to determine which video from which camera should be broadcast to the congregation.

EQUIPMENT SELECTION, SETUP, OPERATION, STORAGE, AND MAINTENANCE

Software

A number of projection programs are available. Some of the more popular choices are listed in the table below. Features vary, and any of them can be used to great effect in worship.

Program	Cost	Operating System
PowerPoint	Inexpensive	Mac OS and Windows OS
Keynote	Inexpensive	Mac OS only
Media Shout	Moderate	Windows OS only
SongShow Plus	Moderate	Windows OS only
Easy Worship	Moderate	Windows OS only
Pro Presenter	Moderate	Mac OS only

Projectors

Projectors come in a variety of types. There are those which are designed for small and large spaces. For a projector which must display over a certain distance, a special lens may need to be purchased. Any modern projector should have input for common audio and video equipment. Although many projectors come with a built-in sound system, except in small meeting rooms, the audio features of the projector will be unused. The video inputs on a modern projector should include RCA audio and video as are found on numerous DVD and VHS tape players, VGA input, and DVI which would be similar to the signal that is sent to a modern digital television. As newer standards evolve, projectors will need to be updated (or converters purchased) which will permit those standards to be displayed.

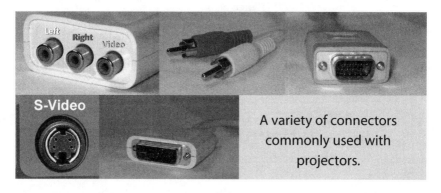

A variety of connectors commonly used with projectors.

Setting Up the Projector

The projector must be mounted where it will display an appropriate size image on the screen to which it projects. As a general rule of thumb, a screen should be from one-third to one-half as wide as the distance from which it is being viewed. For example, in a 40 foot room, the screen should be between 13.3 and 20 feet wide for everyone to view it comfortably. Obviously, this can vary depending on the size of the text projected. For the comfort of the people in the congregation, the screen should not be mounted so low that people cannot see it, or so high that they must hold their heads too far back to view it. The mounting must be secure so there is no danger of falling. If the space is used for other purposes (like a gym) it may need to be protected with a cage (for example, to protect it from stray basketballs). If it is not available, electrical power must be run to the mounting location of the projector. Video lines for each type of signal to be sent to the projector must be run from the projector to the projection booth. If multiple projectors are to be sending different signals, appropriate switch boxes must be obtained as needed. The projector's remote receiver (especially if optical) must be mounted so it can receive signals from the projector's remote control.

Computers

An often-asked question for a projection computer is, "Should I get a laptop or a desktop?" Generally, the answer is, "desktop." Desktop computers generally have more power for less money. A computer used for projection is likely to be permanently installed, so portability is not a concern. Although a laptop would permit the computer to serve double duty, it is not recommended that the projection computer be used for other purposes. Of course, there will be times when there is no choice in this matter, or when portability is a concern. In these cases, a laptop will do a fine job.

A number of people concern themselves with whether a Windows or Apple computer should be used for projection. The software used for projection should be a qualifier as not every software package is compatible with both platforms. (See chart on page 79) Here are some things to consider:

	Windows	Macintosh
Viruses and Malicious Software	More threats	Fewer threats
Userbase	Much larger	Much smaller
Cost	Generally less expensive for low end machines— but cheap machines are not recommended for projection.	Similar to high-end Windows machines.
Reliability	An extended warranty is recommended for any church computer.	
Software Availability	Most major applications run on both Windows and Macintosh. Each platform has some software that will only run on it. If you use platform specific applications like Cakewalk or GarageBand then decide based on the software you will run.	

	Windows	Macintosh
Reading Files from Guests	Compatible with most major file types through OS or commonly installed applications: wmv, mov, aif, waf, mp3, aac, flv, jpg, gif, pdf, txt, rtf, doc, ppt. xls, docx, pptx, xlsx, etc.	
RAM	Put in the maximum the machine will hold for projection.	
Hard Drive	The largest hard drive which can be afforded is recommended. A second hard drive for files (images, videos, etc) is recommended.	
Video	A machine with two video cards is recommended for most projection software. One is used to control the projection and the other is the screen which is projected within the sanctuary.	

DVD and Other Media Players

The best option is to play DVDs from the computer which does all projections. This avoids the problems associated with switching inputs on the projector. Projectors, as of this writing, are not terribly fast at switching, and the process on most machines is error prone. These problems can be avoided by playing graphic, audio, and video media from the computer.

COMMON PROBLEMS: PREVENTION AND SOLUTIONS

Video Plays But Doesn't Show in Sanctuary

In this case it is necessary to trace the signal path from the video source to the projector. Somewhere in the process a problem will be detected. Here are some troubleshooting tips:

- Is the video source (DVD player, Camera, Computer) turned on and playing.

- Are the cables connecting the output of that video source to the projectionist booth in place and working.
- Do the cables run to a switch-box, and if so is the proper video source selected.
- Is the projector turned on?
- Is the projector set to receive input from the appropriate source? Most projectors have multiple inputs and with their remote can be set to any of a number of video inputs. The input must be set to the correction option.

Switching From One Media Playback Device to Another

One of the biggest problems in projection comes when switching from one media playback device to another (for example, a DVD player to a computer). When possible, it is highly desirable to use the same device for all projection. A computer, for example, can play media files (mov, wmv), play DVDs, run PowerPoint or Keynote presentations, and run projection software for lyrics. Things work better when the computer can be used for all projection.

Lyrics Are Not in the System

Occasionally a worship leader will start singing a song not on the song list. Since this is a spur-of-the moment decision, it is common for there to be no lyrics available for the song. If the computer is connected to the Internet, the best option for quickly getting the lyrics into the computer is by connecting software (which will do it) to the licensing organization such as CCLI which administers the song rights. The lyrics can be downloaded and ready for display in a few minutes. It would be a nice training activity for the media coordinator to show how this is done.

Working with Double and Single Monitor Systems (Mirroring)

Many computers setup for display in church have a double monitor system (two video cards). Most new projectionists are not accustomed to working with these systems, so it will fall on the media coordinator to set these up and prepare any special instructions which are needed.

Monitor Resolution Issues

Some projectors support a limited set of computer screen resolutions. In general, the older the projector, the more likely that it will not support modern screen resolutions. The oldest projectors may support only 800×600. (Actually there are projectors that support smaller resolutions, but they are so old as of this writing, they are not likely to still be working). If you connect a modern laptop to one of these older projectors, the screen may not display. You may have to go to the displays (monitors) control panel (system settings) on the laptop and tell it to match the resolution of the projector. It is best to do this before launching any software on the computer.

Connection Issues

Some computers automatically sense when they are connected to a projector and immediately make the necessary connections. Some, however, require the user to press a function key to connect to a projector or external monitor. Most computers requiring the press of a function key, use the key as a toggle. For example, the first press may send the screen to an external monitor and turn off the computer's local monitor. The next press may send the video signal to both. A third press would often send the signal to the computer's screen only. The strategy for connecting to an external monitor may also change based on the version of the operating system running on the computer.

Typically, the chart below shows the standard Function button for activating the second output. To know for sure, look for this (or similar) icon on a function key:

F7	Fn+F4	Fn+F5	Fn+F7	Fn+F8	Fn+F10
Apple	Gateway	Toshiba HP Sony Acer Sharp	Sony (Lenovo)	Dell Epson	Fujitsu

Computer Freezes

In the event of a computer freeze, there is little to do short of restarting the computer. It may be a good idea to have on hand a DVD which can be projected, saying sorry, we are experiencing technical difficulties. When a software freeze occurs, it is particularly troubling because there is no assurance that upon restarting, the problem will be resolved. It is possible that the same circumstance will recur. Still, with computers, restarting them solves a host of problems, so it is worth a try. Common reasons for computer freezes include the following:

- Bugs in the operating system (update to the latest version).
- Bugs in the software (update to the latest version)
- Mismatched software and operating system (you may need to reinstall the operating system and software that was purchased at the time the computer was purchased). (Yes, this contradicts the items above—We all wish computer maintenance was simpler).
- Not enough RAM—this is an easily corrected problem which frequently causes crashes. The projection computer is for the use in the worship service, and as few compromises as possible should be take with it. Expanding the RAM for the computer to the maximum it will hold is a good idea. This will increase the speed and processing capability of the computer.
- Not enough hard drive space—Most modern desktop computers come with hard drives that are large enough for use for years to come. Applications which tend to use a large amount of hard drive space such as video editing may reduce the space available. It is a good idea to start thinking about replacing a hard drive when it is over three years old, or when it reaches 75% of capacity or having a second hard drive installed that stores all multimedia files.
- Hardware problems—hardware problems such as a faulty logic board bad hard drive, failing RAM, or a bad DVD player may well cause repeated crashes. Most computers come with a diagnostic program which can be used to determine if any of these things are happening. If this is the case, it is a good idea to have the computer repaired or replaced before the next service.

CHAPTER 5

Lighting

LIGHTING

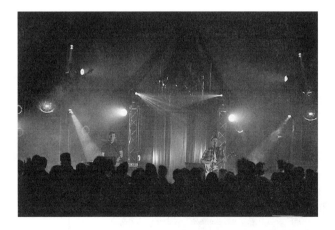

Lighting can be used to set a mood for the worship service and special programs and can have a great impact on the service. This has been a technique used for centuries in the church. Stained glass is an example of the early use of lighting to convey or set a mood.

A stained-glass window.

Modern uses of lighting open up a broader of palette of options for the church. Volunteer positions in lighting may include the following:

Lighting Board Operator: Typically this person sits at a lighting board and controls when and how the various lights which are wired to the board are used.

Lighting Designer: This individual works with other ministers to design the lighting that will be used in the service.

Lighting Set Builder: Many lighting ideas require special placement of lights, and reflective surfaces. At times there will be teams who are charged with setting the lighting, and/or building sets for the lighting.

Some of the commonly used tools of lighting are pictured below. They include stage lights, trusses, racks, light boards, special lighting, spotlights, and effects such as fog, snow, and bubble machines.

Stage lights are usually mounted on trusses or beams on or in front of the platform so they may direct light to various places during a production. In temporary settings such as outside performances or in auditoriums or rooms which don't have trusses and beams, or in instances where lighting is needed where it cannot normally be directed, stage lights may temporarily be mounted on stands.

Stage lights are usually plugged into high wattage power control units which are then controlled by a lighting board.

Spotlights

Spotlights are used to direct attention to specific individuals on the platform. They are well used in dramas and theatrical productions within the church. Spotlights which are always directed to the same point may be mounted on a beam or truss with other stage lighting. These lights usually have few controls (on, off, and various levels of brightness).

Spotlights which may move or follow a character usually are positioned in the back of the church and require an operator. These spotlights include more capabilities and are operated as follows: The spotlight is turned on, pointed toward the desired character or scene. The spotlight stand will permit the light to swivel and move as the action on stage shifts from location to location. The width of the spotlight beam may be set to wide or narrow depending on the effect. Slow changes in the width of a spot may be used to open and close scenes. Most spot lights include filters of different colors so the color of the beam may be adjusted.

Special Lighting

A number of lighting fixtures with automated effects have been developed and may be used for concerts by Christian artists, for youth or other special services. Many of these lighting fixtures generate moving beams or spots of light. In some cases the movement is random, or within a fixed range. In some intelligent fixtures, a microphone monitors the music and the fixture produces different effects depending on the loudness or frequency of the music. Many of these fixtures can be mounted on traditional lighting beams and trusses. Some of these lighting fixtures are shown below.

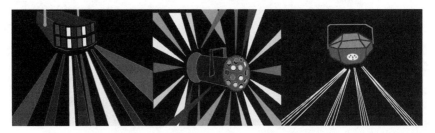

There are a number of dramatic productions in the church which would benefit from special effects such as fog, snow and bubbles. Many Christmas productions could use snow. Many Easter productions would benefit from "fog" in portrayals of the Garden of Gethsemane, the tomb of Jesus, and the ascension. Each of these machines produces output which is generally harmless (bubbles and snow yield soapy water, etc.). All of them, however, do produce some moisture, so delicate musical instruments and other things which might be harmed by moisture may need to be placed out of the way. As a precaution, any individual with breathing difficulties or phobias of enclosures may also need to be directed to a space away from the effects.

Each of these machines requires a specially designed fluid to operate. It is best to always purchase the fog, snow, and bubble solution recommended by the manufacturer. Fluid levels should be checked prior to a performance. Fog machines will NOT operate on water, as might be expected.

Fog and bubble machines are usually positioned near the floor. Snow machines are usually mounted on a lighting beam or truss. Snow machines often come with a remote control which activates them. Fog and bubble machines may have to be turned on by someone close to the machine, or to be wired into a power strip controlled by the lighting board.

CHECKLIST

- Review the service with the person in charge well in advance of the service. Lighting may sometimes require special placement of fixtures, wiring enhancements, or the building of lighting "sets." In some cases, additional equipment (extra spots) may need to be rented or special supplies purchased (different color filters for the various lights). The lighting specialist may be more aware of possibilities for enhancing the production that the person in charge so it is important that the two would meet to brainstorm ideas. A budget may be available within the production for special lighting effects. Regardless, the details concerning any extra costs should be discussed.

- Prior to the rehearsal, all lighting fixtures should be wired and placed as desired for the program. Setup may take some time so this team will need plenty of advanced notice. If the setup is substantial, it is wise to recruit additional team members to assist in this process.

- With lighting teams, rehearsal will be extremely important. Any dress rehearsal or other rehearsals immediately before a production should include the lighting team. These rehearsals are opportunities for the lighting team to practice the effects that have been planned, and to make notes on any special circumstances. In almost every case, rehearsal reveals new insights on how the lighting plan must be executed. The lighting team should be provided with a full copy of the script of any dramatic production and any lighting effects should be marked on the script. Once the equipment being used is in place, new ideas for lighting effects may occur. These should be directed to the person in charge of the production to see if they approve of variations to the lighting plan.

- If the lighting plan includes making adjustments to the placement of lighting fixtures during the performance, then special attention must be given to this. Generally, the idea of moving lighting fixtures during a production is not ideal. If it is necessary, sufficient cooling time must be provided, and enough manpower to move the fixtures without damage must be available. It may be that members of the production can be recruited for this task. Moving the fixtures should be rehearsed and there should be no question about who is to do it. More commonly, reflective services used in lighting may be moved as any other set element is moved. Sometimes the performers themselves wear white cotton in front of black lights, and the performers are the set. Sometimes reflective strips of cloth are draped or stretched over set elements which can be easily moved.

- After the production, power down any equipment as necessary and permit it to cool before moving it. Put away any equipment as necessary. Any permanent fixtures need to be turned off. Any temporary fixtures should be placed in appropriate storage after a production.

LIGHTING IDEAS

Having a creative lighting team who can associate lighting options with action in the drama is invaluable. Some basic ideas are given in the tables below, but, again, a creative team will brainstorm much more.

Full Light Communicates

- Brightness of day
- Community
- Large groups
- Energy

Dim Lights Communicate

- Intimacy
- Quiet
- Reflection
- Romance

Colored Lights Can Mean Many Things Depending on Context

- Red—anger, passion, love, blushing
- Blue—cool, dark, night, quiet (not loud), soft (not hard), blues, depression
- Yellow—brightness, hope, awakening,
- Green—springtime, hope, envy, jealousy

Changes in Lighting Can Mean Many Things
Dark to Light
- The play begins
- Sunrise
- Hope is rising
- A character has achieved enlightenment

Light to Dark

- The play or scene ends
- Sunset
- Hope is lost
- A character is facing difficult times

Spotlight Operation

- A spotlight serves to focus attention on a character or characters.
- A spotlight may close slightly to show:
- A character's individual thoughts
- A character's selfishness
- A character's calculating plans
- A spotlight may close completely to indicate the close of a scene.
- A spotlight may open to show:
- A character's setting
- A character's role or place in the community
- A character's broadening perspective
- A character's interactions with others
- A spotlight may open to full to indicate the closing of a scene.

TROUBLESHOOTING

The lighting person should always know where the circuit breaker board for the church is located, and how to find and reset a circuit that may be blown.

One of the biggest troubleshooting issues with lighting systems is solved by checking all bulbs to make certain they are functional. Any which are not working should be replaced. Because many of the bulbs in the lighting system are located on or near the ceiling of the sanctuary, having a ladder or lift in storage nearby is a great help. It may be necessary to rent a lift from time to time to install new fixtures, replace bulbs, and correct any wiring issues.

A modern lighting system depends on careful wiring. Problems with permanently mounted fixtures generally require an electrician to correct.

Temporary lighting often uses extension cords. Be sure to choose those which are rated to carry sufficient wattage for the lighting being operated. Often temporary lighting fixtures are run through power strips which have a built in circuit breaker. Older power strips with fuses should be replaced. Fuses are too difficult to replace under pressure. If temporary lighting fails, here are some things to check:

- Are they plugged in?
- Is the outlet known to have power? If not, reset the circuit breakers.
- Are any power strips leading to the lighting turned on?
- Are any circuit breakers on the power strips leading to the lighting blown? If so, reset them.
- If there is a switch on the lighting fixture is it turned on?
- Are the bulbs in the fixture functional?

Another vulnerable spot in any lighting system are dimmer switches. Frequently these devices fail, or generate noise which is picked up in the sound system. Replacing failed switches is easily accomplished. If a dimmer switch is suspected as a source of noise in a sound system (you can tell because the hum or noise appears as the switch is operated), the problem can often be solved by relocating the dimmer switch, or the lines that it controls. Audio systems should generally be plugged into "power cleaner" strips which filter out problems caused by other electrical equipment in the church.

CHAPTER 6

Audio Recording

WHY RECORD AUDIO?

Audio recordings of church services are made for a number of reasons. Sometimes members are away but want to follow the teaching presented in a given sermon series. Perhaps there are individuals with health or transportation issues who cannot attend. A recording of the service helps them stay connected. Sometimes members are moved by a particular message and want copies to play again, or to give to those that they know would be encouraged by the message. The pastor or worship leader may want a copy of the service to study to see what they can do better. Of course, if the church has a broadcast ministry either on local radio or over the Internet, an audio recording will be required.

EQUIPMENT

Once a decision is made to record the service a number of additional factors come into consideration. Additional equipment may be required. A CD recorder mounted in a rack and receiving a signal from the mixing board provides a quick method of making live recordings of the services.

The advantage of this process is ease of use. To record the service, the soundboard operator puts blank media into the recorder and presses the record button. Depending on the recorder, and media being used, it may be necessary for the person to press a "mark track" button between sections of the service. It may be desired that some parts of the service are not recorded. If that is the case, the pause button should be pressed until it is time to record again. At the end of the service it may be necessary to press a button to "finalize" the recording. If there is no "mark track" feature on the recorder, the service can be divided into sections in post production, but the most convenient time to do it is during the service. Sometimes the "pause" button is used as a "mark track" button. In these cases, momentarily pressing pause and then resume creates the mark. Marking the sections of the recording requires that the sound technician be alert and give attention to this process.

The disadvantage of using a dedicated recorder like this is that the recording is an exact recording of the mix sent to the house speakers unless the recorder is fed from an auxiliary or matrix output on the sound console. For the sermon or spoken parts of the service, the main output should provide an excellent solution. For the music, however, the main output may yield less desirable results. Even with the best sound technicians, it is difficult to get a live mix to sound as good as one which is mixed and edited in post production. Given the limitations of this recording setup, a reasonably good recording can be produced. It is also worthy of note, that some licensing organizations cover live recordings in a way that they do not cover recordings mixed or edited in post-production.

To improve the quality of the music recorded during a service, and to do multi-track editing after the service is over, an additional mixing board will be needed. The signals from a digital mixing board may sometimes be stored on an internal hard drive in the board, but could also be sent to professional audio software on an attached computer. When selecting digital audio software to use for recording services, reliability is a key consideration. Many top-of-the line programs are "cutting-edge" and are consequently prone to crashes. It is strongly advised that a live recording of every service using a CD recorder be made, even when the service is also being recorded using a digital mixing board.

A multi-track recording will also be dependent on having a separate feed to the recording board which is accomplished by a splitter. This allows the recording operator to adjust levels and mixes that are independent from the house soundboard.

MICROPHONES

In a regular service, acoustic instruments such as the organ, brass instruments, or drum set may not be miked at all. If the service is to be recorded, microphones will need to be placed so that those instruments can also be heard. In a regular service, the congregational singing and reaction to the elements of the service may be a significant part of the experience. If these audible responses are to be captured, microphones will need to be placed where they can be recorded. Because these are sounds that are already present in the regular service, it may be that signals from these microphones run through channels on the soundboard that are recorded but not amplified.

VOLUNTEERS

The decision to record may require additional volunteers for the various parts of the process, or at least additional duties for the soundboard operator.

RECORDING BOARD OPERATOR

Ideally, the soundboard is a digital board with either the ability to record internally or to send digital signals (optical, firewire or USB) to a computer for recording. The soundboard operator generally does what they normally would, with the possible exception of having to start recording either on the board itself or on a nearby computer. In some cases, a separate recording and soundboard may be setup. In these cases, signals will need to be shared between the two boards and a separate operator will be required.

COMPUTER AND SOFTWARE OPERATOR

If signals from a digital mixing board are routed to a computer for recording, the computer needs to be configured to match the incoming signals. Typically this includes creating a new document for recording, adding tracks for every incoming channel of sound the digital mixing board is sending, setting each of those tracks to listen to the appropriate input channel of the attached mixing board and adjusting the input levels of each incoming channel. Fortunately much of this process can be done once, then a template matching the soundboard can be saved to use for every service. If a template is to be used, the computer operator should be trained to open and use it properly (so the template is still available for the next service).

SOUND EDITOR

This person does mechanical edits of the service, makes it fit into the time slot needed (30 minutes for example), adds intro and outro material.

MUSIC EDITOR

This person may need full production skills and remixes the tracks in post-production. This person should have a musical ear, and should be able to select the best effects (reverb, equalization, compression.) to enhance the recording. This person will need to have an ear for problems and eliminate those from the mix (for example, an out of tune guitar).

CHECKLIST FOR AUDIO RECORDING

- Turn on any necessary equipment for recording. The exact equipment to be used will be individually determined by each church. It is likely that a stand-alone recorder or a digital soundboard with a computer will be used.
- Place the media for recording in the recording equipment. Usually this is as simple as placing a CD or DVD in the recording equipment, or making sure there is plenty of hard drive space for recording. A large collection of high quality blank CDs or DVDs should be on hand. When the supply reaches a level that will only last a few weeks, report the shortage to the media coordinator, or buy additional media.
- Check the signal levels coming into the recording equipment and set them appropriately. Regardless of the equipment being used to record the service, it is essential that the levels being recorded are checked. If a signal is too loud, part of the sound will be lost during the recording process. It could render a great recording unusable. If the signal is too low, other problems may occur. For example, the signal can be amplified after recording with editing equipment, however, if there is

any noise on the line, it will also be amplified. It may be that the ratio of noise to the signal is too great for the recording to be used.

- Start and stop the recording at the appropriate times in the service. Because of copyright concerns, concerns about privacy, attempts to produce a higher quality recording with fewer awkward moments, etc., it may be necessary to insure that parts of a service are not recorded. Your leaders will make you aware if this is a consideration. For a discussion of copyright, see below. Unwanted sections of the service can also be removed during editing.

- Depending on the solution used for recording, mixing could occur at different times. Mixing would not be necessary if the signal from the soundboard is being recorded exactly as is. If the service is being recorded with a multi-track recorder, it may be possible to mix the recording during the service. The best results are obtained when there is enough time to mix and edit the tracks after the service.

- After the service, save the recording, or finalize any media as needed (burn the CD). This becomes the archival CD for the service, and the source for materials which will be produced for broadcast or further distribution.

- After any necessary editing, provide copies of the service in an appropriate format to the person or persons in charge of broadcast or Web services, and file a copy in the church's archives. Depending on how the responsibilities for recording and editing are assigned, there may be some light to heavy editing required.

- Make copies of the media for those who request or purchase a copy of the service. If copies are given to members of the congregation immediately after the service, it is usually best to give them only the sermon, with any references to copyrighted lyrics, poems, or media deleted. If materials are to be given to them immediately after the service, it will be necessary to have duplication equipment on hand. A more common strategy might be for orders for the materials to be placed on one Sunday and picked up (after editing and duplication) the following Sunday.

- Turn off equipment as necessary.

AUDIO STUDIO WITHIN THE CHURCH

Some churches have radio or other programs which consist of devotions or things other than their primary service. If this is the case, a studio may be setup within the church for recording those programs. A studio like this usually includes microphones as needed, a digital to audio converter box, a computer, a couple of monitors and professional audio editing software. A typical studio setup is pictured below. The studio below also includes an electronic keyboard, which can be used for MIDI recording. See the sidebar on page 104, for more information about recording MIDI and digital audio.

RECORDING

The studio above shows a two channel audio to digital converter box with one microphone (a second could easily be plugged in for interviews). A church studio may need more channels and these are easily achieved by the addition of a digital mixing board such as the one pictured on the following page.

A digital mixing board expands your recording options.

Recording MIDI and Digital Audio

Most recording is done using the audio signals from microphones or instruments. Modern keyboards, drum machines and numerous other devices also send MIDI signals. MIDI stands for musical instrument digital interface. MIDI signals are compact compared to digital audio signals. Digital audio signals describe the exact manner in which a speaker must move to recreate the sound that was recorded. Every playback of a digital audio file yields a very similar result. MIDI, on the other hand, is more like a list of which notes should be played and when. This list is sent to a keyboard, sound module, virtual synthesizer, or other MIDI instrument and that instrument produces the sounds. Depending on the instrument to which MIDI signals are sent, the sounds can vary widely. One of the great advantages of MIDI is that it records a performance in a manner which can be edited in numerous ways. Wrong notes can be removed, missing notes can be added, and rhythmic errors can be corrected. New instrument sounds can be assigned to the various tracks. Individual notes within a chord that were played to loudly or softly can be corrected. While some of these edits are possible when editing digital audio, none are possible to the extent they are in MIDI recordings. Once a MIDI recording is edited to satisfaction, and a desired sound from a MIDI instrument or virtual instrument on a computer have been achieved, the MIDI recording is then converted (recorded) as digital audio so it can be mixed with the rest of the recording, saved as an audio file (mp3, wav, etc.), or burned to a CD.

GEAR

A number of companies make digital mixing boards, audio interfaces, or computer cards that can be used in the process of recording.

- ProTools   http://www.digidesign.com
- M-Audio   http://www.m-audio.com
- SoundBlaster   http://www.soundblaster.com
- Korg   http://www.korg.com
- Yamaha   http://www.yamaha.com
- Roland   http://www.roland.com

RECORDING AND EDITING HARDWARE AND SOFTWARE

A number of different kinds of software can be used to record. All are similar enough that they accomplish the same tasks, with minor differences in interface and features. The one that a church selects will depend more on preferences of the people in the ministry there than big differences in features. Here are a few examples:

Audacity

Audacity is a free, open source program that does an outstanding job of recording, especially considering the price. It is completely capable of mono and stereo recording and, with the proper interface can record multiple channels simultaneously. On some operating systems, external audio to digital converter boxes can be used with Audacity for high quality multi-track recordings. On others, however, good results can be achieved on stereo recordings when using the built-in audio card of the computer.

Sonar

Cakewalk's Sonar is a Windows-only digital audio recording software program. It has the overwhelming majority of the market share for casual (home-studio) Windows users. Sonar's Home Studio and Home Studio XL are the entry-level products offered by the company. Sonar Producer and Studio are the company's two professional programs. Sonar Studio comes with various hardware, depending on one's recording needs. The products can record multiple tracks at a time.

GarageBand

GarageBand is a Macintosh-only digital audio recording software program. It has the overwhelming majority of the market share for casual (home-studio) Macintosh users. Its great advantage (which probably isn't all that useful in most church settings except by songwriters) is a wonderful collection of royalty free loops. Any songs composed with Garageband, and harmonized with its loops may be distributed freely as original compositions[1]. GarageBand, with an appropriate audio interface and powerful enough computer can record multiple tracks at a time.

Logic

Apple publishes a family of programs for digital audio ranging from Logic Express to Logic Pro. These programs run on the Macintosh only. Each of these programs has a collection of plug-ins that permits professional-level audio editing. Logic can record multiple tracks at a time. As of this writing, Logic Pro includes all of the Garage Band loops, plus all Jam Packs (sound loops) that Apple has created. Logic can also open and edit GarageBand files.

---

[1] The GarageBand software license agreement says: "GarageBand Software. You may use the Apple and third party audio loop content (Audio Content), contained in or otherwise included with the Apple Software, on a royalty-free basis, to create your own original music compositions or audio projects. You may broadcast and/or distribute your own music compositions or audio projects that were created using the Audio Content, however, individual audio loops may not be commercially or otherwise distributed on a standalone basis, nor may they be repackaged in whole or in part as audio samples, sound effects or music beds." From http://support.apple.com/kb/HT2931

Steinberg Cubase

The manufacturer of Cubase produces an excellent family of cross-platform digital audio software. The software ranges from Sequel to Cubase PRO. Sequel is a unique program with a large collection of pre-recorded loops and is similar in many ways to GarageBand. Cubase PRO is Steinberg's top-of-the-line recording software. The quality of their product is excellent. Cubase can record multiple tracks at a time.

Mackie Tracktion

Mackie Tracktion is a Windows-only digital audio recording program. Its advantage is that it comes with many Mackie mixing boards and it is designed to interface digital mixing boards with a computer and provide a simple means of recording raw tracks for later post production. Its disadvantage is the relatively smaller community of users. Mackie Tracktion comes with many Mackie digital soundboards. Recording multiple tracks simultaneously is one of its strengths.

Avid ProTools

ProTools has become the industry standard for recording professional digital audio. ProTools includes a family of products ranging from ProTools LE which comes with the M-Box, a two track audio to digital converter, through ProTools HD which comes with Digidesign multi-track Digital mixing boards. Pro Tools software and is designed only to work with Pro Tools recording interfaces.

Digital Performer

This Macintosh-only software has a healthy band of adherents who use it to make outstanding recordings. Digital Performer, with an appropriate audio interface and powerful enough computer can record multiple tracks at a time.

Many of the titles listed above also provide hardware interfaces that work seamlessly with the software. Although it is into required in every instance, it is a more seamless process to integrate the hardware and software of the same manufacturer and the support is less hassle because you only have one vendor to work with.

DUPLICATION EQUIPMENT

CDs and DVDs can be duplicated one at a time using a computer; however, this solution is time consuming and would not be sufficient except for the smallest ministries. A number of companies make CD and DVD duplicating equipment which can produce 10 to 100 CDs in one pass.

Operation of those devices that make ten copies at a time is typically as follows: A copy of the CD or DVD is loaded into the device's hard drive from an original CD or DVD. Blank CDs or DVDs are placed in the device's ten or more CD/DVD writers. When the start button is pressed, the device burns the CDs or DVDs simultaneously. Older models of this equipment actually had the original CD or DVD in the top drive and burned exact copies while reading from the top drive.

Operation of those devices that make 100 copies at a time is typically as follows. These devices may often be combined with printers which can print directly to the face of a CD (special print-ready CD media is required). The blank CDs are placed in a bin which looks similar to a juke box. An arm picks up each CD one at a time, inserts it into the printing and burning slot. When finished, the arm drops the CD into a bin on the other side of the device.

Because these devices often have to have information on how to print the CD cover, they often interface with a computer, rather than run independently. If CD Printing is not a part of the process of duplication, a separate CD printer may need to be obtained.

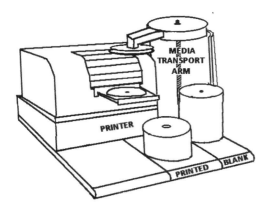

AUDIO EDITING TECHNIQUES

Once a service is recorded, many kinds of audio editing may be done. The list below lists many common edits.

Cut and Paste

Every digital audio editing program has the facility for cut-and-paste editing. A selection of a section of audio is made and may be cut (Edit Menu>Cut) from the original. The software may have setting to determine if all other audio is moved in to fill the space, or if the cut audio creates an empty space in the recording. If the audio is moved, it is usually important to cut from all tracks to maintain alignment after the cut. Any audio which has been cut, is stored in the computer's temporary memory and may be pasted elsewhere in the document. Again, the mode of the software may determine if the location where it is pasted moves existing audio to the end of the audio being pasted, or if the audio being pasted replaces the existing audio. If this audio track will be synced later with a video recording, an uncut version should be maintained.

Copy and Paste

This is the same as cut and paste but the audio is not removed when copied.

Other Editing Effects

The menu shown to the left is from Audacity, but many digital audio programs have similar editing capabilities.

Amplify—This makes the recorded track louder. In some digital audio software, it is possible to amplify a signal so much that clipping occurs. That is something that should be avoided. Observe any warnings in the software to prevent this.

Bass Boost—This is a frequency equalization effect that increases the volume of the lower frequencies.

Change Pitch—This effect changes the pitch of a recorded note or voice. It can be used to change one note to another note, in some cases to tune an out-of-tune note, or to make a person sound like a chipmunk. This feature changes pitch but not speed.

Change Speed—This effect changes the pitch and speed of a recorded note or voice. This is much like playing a 33 RPM record at 45 or 78 RPM.

Change Tempo—This effect changes the duration of a recording (say from 32 minutes to exactly 30 minutes). It does so without changing pitch.

Click Removal—This function scans the track looking for sudden spikes and removes them.

Compressor—This effect scans a track and reduces the volume of any sounds found over a specified threshold volume level. Vocal mics in particular, tend to use a greater dynamic range than a listener is accustomed to hearing. Compressing the track and then amplifying the entire track makes the track more dynamically natural.

Echo—This effect copies the existing track, processes the sound to make it quieter, then mixes it with the original copy of the track, but at a specified interval later. The number of "echoes" and their intensity can sometimes be controlled.

Equalization—This effect permits the editor to adjust low, middle, or high frequencies (with great control).

Fade In—This effect takes a selected section of a track and reduces the volume to zero at the start and gradually increases the volume to full level by the end of the selection.

Fade Out—This function takes a selected section of a track and gradually reduces the volume to zero from the start to the end of the selection.

FFT Filter—This effect performs equalization using a different interface.

Invert—This function simply reverses the polarity of a signal. In other words, if the original sound moved a speaker in by a certain amount, the inverted signal would move it out by the same amount.

Noise Removal—This effect scans a selected portion of the track to learn what kind of noise is in the track. On a second pass, it attempts to remove all such sounds from the track.

Normalize—This effect amplifies the audio in the track or selection to the loudest possible level without clipping, or losing data while keeping the track audio relative to the original.

Nyquist Prompt—This command permits the user to manipulate the sound using a number of preprogrammed commands defined according to the Nyquist audio programming language. For more details, see http://www-2.cs.cmu.edu/~rbd/doc/nyquist/root.html.

Phaser—This effect creates a copy of the original track and mixes it with the original, but slightly out of phase. It creates some interesting, although generally unpredictable results in the track volume. The effect has been standardized to a large degree and included on many guitar effects pedals.

Repeat—This effect copies and pastes the selection so that it occurs twice.

Reverse—This effect reverses the selected waveform. It is probably beyond human perception, but some claim there are subliminal messages played backwards and mixed into some music. Those edits could be done with this tool.

Wahwah—This effect applies increasing and decreasing frequency resonance settings to an existing sound, creating a "wah wah" effect. The effect has also been standardized and included on many guitar effects pedals.

Cross Fade In—This effect combines two tracks so that the first fades out, while the second fades in. The implementation in Audacity is a bit unusual, more like a regular fade in.

Cross Fade Out—This effect combines two tracks so that the first fades in, while the second fades out. The implementation in Audacity is a bit unusual, more like a regular fade out.

DC Bias Removal—Sometimes a recording produces a wave which is not centered on zero. Remove DC bias, balances the wave so that the center is closer to zero.

Delay—This effect creates one or more copies of the original signal, and mixes it with the original but starting at a later time. It is an echo effect.

High Pass Filter—This effect provides a type of equalization, where all low frequencies can be reduced or eliminated.

Low Pass Filter—This effect provides a type of equalization, where all high frequencies can be reduced or eliminated.

Tremolo—This effect applies a rapid variation in amplitude to the sound.

COPYRIGHT AND LICENSING

U. S. Copyright law permits the making of one archival copy of the service, so there is never any concern about whether it is legal to record a service. Further duplication or distribution of the service requires a more detailed consideration of copyrights. The parts of the service that were created by the pastor and church staff are usually free from copyright concerns. For example, the sermon should be predominantly free of copyright concerns. However, when the Pastor quotes a poem, lyrics from a song, or plays an excerpt from a commercial CD or DVD or otherwise uses copyrighted material, those portions of the service may be subject to copyright laws which govern how duplication and distribution may occur. Whether this would be the case depends in large part on the scope of the materials used, how they were used (parody, review, or criticism may be permitted), etc. Also, certain parts of the worship service are almost certain to contain materials that are subject to copyright. For example, most of the worship music cannot be legally reproduced unless permission or licenses are obtained to do so. A number of organizations simplify copyright concerns for worshipers.

Church Copyright Licensing International (CCLI) offers an affordable license to churches based on the size of their congregation. Under the terms of the CCLI license, license holders' rights are defined as follows:

What You Can Do

Print songs, hymns and lyrics in bulletins, programs, liturgies and song sheets for use in congregational singing.

Create your own customized songbooks or hymnals for use in congregational singing.

Create overhead transparencies, slides or use any other format whereby song lyrics are visually projected (such as computer graphics and projection) for use in congregational singing.

Arrange, print and copy your own arrangements (vocal and instrumental) of songs used for congregational singing, where no published version is available.

Record your worship services (audio or video) provided you only record live music. Accompaniment tracks cannot be reproduced. You may charge up to $4 each for audiocassette tapes and CDs, and $12 each for videotapes and DVDs.

What You Cannot Do

Photocopy or duplicate octavos, cantatas, musicals, handbell music, keyboard arrangements, vocal scores, orchestrations or other instrumental works.

Translate songs into another language. This can only be done with the approval of the respective publisher.

Rent, sell or lend copies made under the license to groups outside the church or to other churches. (It is okay to distribute recordings to shut-ins, missionaries or others outside the church.)

Assign or transfer the license to another church or group without CCLI's approval.

From the CCLI website, July, 2009—http://www.ccli.com/WhatWeOffer/ WhatYouCanDo.aspx

Note that the CCLI license does not include permission to broadcast copyrighted materials through radio, television, or the Internet. For these and other rights not included in the list above, you may need to work with one of the music licensing organizations which represent songwriters around the country:

ASCAP (American Society of Composers, Authors, and Publishers): ASCAP is an organization of composers, songwriters, lyricists, and music publishers of every kind of music. The organization licenses the music of its members to those who wish to perform in public. The organization distributes the royalties collected to its members. More information about ASCAP licenses is found here http://www.ascap.com.

BMI (Broadcast Music, Inc.): Broadcast Music, Inc. collects license fees from businesses, restaurants, government organizations, radio stations, television stations, Websites, and others that use music then distributes those royalties to the songwriters, composers and music publishers who are members of BMI. BMI offers a number of licenses tailored for specific uses. Details are found at http://www.bmi.com.

SESAC was originally the Society of European Stage Authors and Composers. Today it represents a much wider clientele and is simply known as SESAC. SESAC's role is very similar to ASCAP and BMI in that they are in the business of representing songwriters and publishes and collecting royalties for the public performance of their works. For more information about their works see http://www.sesac.com

Harry Fox Agency is a licensing organization established by the National Music Publisher's Association. Harry Fox Agency offers two specific licenses for copyrighted materials:

Mechanical Licenses which permit the use of copyrighted musical compositions on CDs, records, tapes, and certain digital configurations.

Digital Licenses which permit the use of copyrighted materials for permanent digital downloads, limited downloads, interactive streaming, and ringtones.

For additional information, see http://www.hfa.com

Bottom Line

The sound editor may need to remove copyrighted portions of the service, or initiate the licensing process to use copyrighted materials before duplicating or distributing the service by copies or broadcast.

There are generally a number of creative individuals in a church including many who have written original songs. Often, these individuals would be pleased for their materials to be used in the ministry of the church, or for the promotion it provides to their work. Professional recordings of these songs may yield nice royalty-free materials for the ministry of the local church. However, it should be noted that even though they wrote the song if they have signed off the publishing to another company or they have a co-writer who has done the same then permission must still be granted before the song can be reproduced.

COMMON RECORDING PROBLEMS: PREVENTION AND SOLUTIONS

Signal Not Reaching the Recording Hardware or Software?

- Follow the signal path from the source to the recording device. Check any cables and connectors being used. Check any instruments being used.
- Check to see that level is appearing on the signal lights
- If there are audio interfaces in the recording chain, restart them being careful that it will not produce an audible POP in the speakers. It may be necessary to turn down or off the speakers before restarting the audio interfaces.
- If the recording device is a computer, check to make sure the correct audio interface and drives are being used. Make certain the operating system preferences are set correctly.
- If the recording device is a stand-alone recorder, check to see if the correct input is selected.

Signal Too Soft or Too Loud?

- The level of a signal to be recorded could vary greatly depending on whether the source is a microphone, instrument, keyboard or audio device. Ideally the hardware being used to record the sound has a preamplifier in which the signal levels can be adjusted. If so, adjust it.
- Audio interfaces and digital mixing boards typically have a knob which can be turned to adjust the audio input. Adjust as necessary.
- Computers, especially connected through the computer's soundcard, typically have a software adjustment to the input level. Adjust as necessary.

CHAPTER 7

Video Recording

VIDEO RECORDING AND MIXING

 A church might want to record their services for a number of reasons. Perhaps the recordings will be distributed to "shut-ins." Perhaps members will want copies of the service for their personal devotions, or to give to friends and family. Perhaps the services will be broadcast or distributed over the Internet. Regardless, it is common for a church to have decided that for these or other reasons, the service is to be recorded. These are some of the positions that will be available in the video recording ministry.

Camera Operator

This person's primary responsibility is to keep the camera trained on the appropriate area of the service. Prior to the service, if necessary, the camera will be white balanced. If it is deemed appropriate by an editor, the cameras may all train their signal on a clapboard prior to the beginning of the service so that, if other timing mechanisms fail, the footage from various sources can easily be synchronized.

The signal from the camera can be recorded in the camera itself, or at another location. If the camera is to record the service, the camera operator will be responsible for inserting media in the camera (if required). If the camera records to permanent media such as a built-in hard drive, the camera operator will be responsible for checking to be sure that there is enough space to record the service. If necessary, the camera operator will erase previous services that have been archived to make room for upcoming services. If the camera operator is to be a member of a team of camera operators under the direction of a director, they will complete a soundcheck of the headphone or communication system that connects them to one another and to the director.

Cameras should generally be mounted on a stand for recording a service. Perhaps one camera operator with a handheld can be used for custom shots (for example, zooming in on the keyboard players fingers) but most of the shots used will be from the permanently mounted cameras. One or more cameras may be mounted on boom stands (or crane stands) for special shots. These will require training as the camera must be mounted in the boom, and angled correctly for appropriate use. Even then, the boom only gives useful results over a part of its range. The producer and video monitor on the floor near this camera can help achieve the best results.

Producer/Director/Mixer

This person typically works in an environment with multiple cameras. They usually have the signals from a number of cameras coming into a video mixing board and select which one to use for each moment of the program. They also select the types of transitions that will be used when switching from one camera to another. In the case of church services, the cross-dissolve transition is by far the most common. It is used for virtually every transition, unless there is a good reason to use another. This person may also instruct the camera operators on the kind of shot they should make. Frequently, to give the video a sense of motion, the producer would instruct specific cameramen to execute slow and fast zooms. In concerts, attention to different performers may be given, or focus on the performance techniques of a specific instrumentalist. In concerts, slow transitions between a worship leader, and the congregation, or a wide shot of the stage are common.

Post Production Editor

This person will need expertise in video editing software and post-production experience. This person does mechanical edits of the service. They may need to edit the video footage so that it includes the intro and outro materials and so that it fits into the time slot needed (30 minutes for example). If there is a separately mixed audio track that will be used instead of the audio that was recorded with the video, this person will have to coordinate with the audio person so that problems in syncing the two are not created by previous editing of the audio and video. The post-production editor will sync the audio and video tracks. This person will be responsible for removing any embarrassing moments, any awkward silences, and any material for which there is not permission or license to broadcast.

SOFTWARE

There are two commonly used entry level video editing programs. iMovie comes free with every modern Macintosh. It permits the easy addition of video footage, photos with panning and zooming, titles, transitions, video effects, custom audio tracks, and sound effects. Windows MovieMaker comes free with every modern installation of Windows. It permits the easy addition of video footage, titles, transitions, video effects, custom audio tracks.

Two professional-level video edition programs are commonly used. FinalCut Pro runs on Apple Macintosh computers only. It contains a suite of programs for various purposes. FinalCut Pro itself is where most of the video editing is done including cut and paste editing, timeline adjustments, and transitions. There are separate programs for making titles, editing sound, creating custom DVDs, and compressing the video using specific video standards. Adobe Premier runs on Windows computers only. It is similar in function to FinalCut Pro and contains a large number of pre-built effects. Both Adobe Premiere and FinalCut Pro software are professional level programs with a steep learning curve. Adobe Premiere or FinalCut Pro will be required for many kinds of video editing.

A number of procedures for the duplication of video and audio files are the same for both. Also, copyright information for video and audio are the same. See chapter 6 for information on these topics.

CHECKLIST FOR VIDEO RECORDING

- Power on any cameras and necessary equipment for recording. Among the items needing power may be cameras, video mixing boards, communication systems, computers, and special lighting.
- If required by the camera, make any adjustments necessary for white balance. Many cameras send signals with a slightly different tint. If the camera permits it, completing a white balance by training the camera on a white reflective surface and executing white balance options will help the camera accurately capture white as well as color.
- If the recording is to take place in a camera, check to confirm that the media for recording is in the camera. If the capacity of the media will be exceeded during the service, make certain that additional media is on hand. Cameras use a variety of media for recording depending on their age. Many types of video tape are used, as are mini compact disks, and hard drives. Removable media such as tape and DVDs should be placed in the camera before beginning. Permanent media such as hard drives should be checked for enough space for recording.

- If the signal from the camera is being directed to a mixing board then check the signal from the camera to the mixing board, and check to make certain that any software or hardware is appropriately configured for recording. The producer should be able to see the input from the camera on their monitor at all times. The producer should also confirm that the signals being sent to the mixing board are being recorded either on the boar itself or on an attached computer.
- If multiple cameras are being used, check the communication system between the producer and the camera operators. Check communications in both directions. Check both headphones and microphones for every camera operator and for the producer.
- Start recording once the service is in progress. If multiple cameras are being used, camera operators should follow the directions of the "producer." The advantage of the multiple-camera system is that a sense of action can be added to the message by switching between different views. Often effects can be used such as slow cross fades of two camera signals which yields a nice effect. The producer has the responsibility for directing these shots.
- Depending on the solution used for recording, mixing may or may not be necessary, and could occur either at this time or after the recording is complete. If the camera signals are being directed into a video mixing board, it is very possible to create high quality recordings in real time. If the cameras are individually recording the service, the various views can be mixed after the service using professional video editing software. Sometimes when a real-time mixing effect fails (perhaps someone on screen yawns), it may be possible to replace that with footage from a wide shot where things are not obvious, or a shot of the choir showing someone else's better reaction.
- After the service, save the recording, or finalize any media as needed (burn to DVD). Any recordings made in the camera using DVD media may require finalizing to be used elsewhere. Any cameras saving their output to a hard drive need to be turned in to whoever will be editing video for the service.

- After any necessary editing, provide copies of the service in an appropriate format to the person or persons in charge of broadcast or Web services, and file a copy in the church's archives. Depending on how the responsibilities for recording and editing are assigned, there may be some light to heavy editing required.
- Make copies of the media for those who request or purchase a copy of the service. It is unlikely that copies of the service can be given to members of the congregation immediately after the service. Video editing and rendering is usually a time consuming process. In almost any cases where congregants want a video copy of the service, it is best to have them complete an order form and provide a copy of the service the following week. In the editing process prior to distribution, it is necessary to address any copyright, licensing, and privacy concerns.
- Power down any equipment as necessary.

VIDEO STUDIO WITHIN THE CHURCH

Some churches have television or other programs which consist of devotions or things other than their primary service. If this is the case, a video studio may be setup within the church for recording those programs. A video studio usually includes special furniture for the broadcast (news desk, round table, sofa, etc.), special lighting, multiple cameras, a video mixing board, and a computer for recording the program. Often equipment used in the recording of the sanctuary services can be wired to record from either location. Some video studios are large enough for a small audience. Larger audiences can be accommodated in the sanctuary if needed.

TROUBLESHOOTING

Fortunately most video equipment is quite stable so once the connections are made, everything usually works well.

LOST SIGNAL

If a camera disappears from the video mixing board, it usually means the media is being swapped out, it became unplugged, or it was switched off. If none of these are the case, then it is necessary to follow the signal path from the camera to the mixing board.

BROKEN EQUIPMENT

Some video equipment will break from time to time, and the only thing to do is to have it repaired or replaced. Symptoms of problems with a camera should be obvious (video flickering, sound that doesn't record, etc.).

CHAPTER 8

Broadcasting

There are many options available today for churches which wish to broadcast their services. Local radio and television channels sometimes make time available. Cable television frequently permits local broadcasting. Web and Internet technologies permit broadcasts through a number of means including prerecorded and live broadcast.

BROADCASTING

One of the simplest forms of broadcasting is posting a recorded service to the church's Website. A church with a Web page may have everything needed already in place. A video recording can be easily converted to Internet friendly file formats, such as Flash, MOV or WMV, and uploaded to the church's Web page. An HTML page describing the service and connecting to the movie files is created and posted. That's it. If a visitor to the Website can follow links to the video page, they can watch each week's service. See Chapter 9 for more details.

YouTube is a free online service where members can post videos which anyone can view. YouTube accepts a number of video formats, but this author has had the greatest success uploading AVI files. AVI files are an older video standard with little if any compression. YouTube then compresses the audio and video into an FLV (Flash Video) file, which can be played on any computer with a recent installation of Flash. The greatest advantages of posting video to YouTube are that YouTube is convenient, popular, and free. The greatest disadvantages are the loss of video and audio quality during compression although this is constantly improving. Another disadvantage of YouTube is that it is commonly used for items of a non-religious nature. In other words, it might be easy to stumble across something on YouTube that might not be appropriate for a Christian audience. YouTube does offer a feature which helps avoid this problem. It's videos are generally offered with an "embed" code, which lets them be placed within Web pages on other sites, a church Website for example. When YouTube videos are embedded, they do not display advertising around the video. Regardless, it is impossible to control the videos that will show up as similar or recommended, after a person views a YouTube video. Normally, the videos suggested are similar and appropriate, but again, this is not always the case.

MySpace is a popular Website for bands. It permits members to post audio and video. A number of Christian bands promote their music there. Like similar sites, it compresses audio and video, but the quality is reasonably good. Like similar sites, it may expose visitors to inappropriate content through advertising and the writings of its members. Like YouTube, anyone may watch MySpace videos. Finally, like YouTube, MySpace limits the size and length of videos that can be posted.

Facebook is a popular social networking Website. Its members can post videos which are available to specified populations (limited groups or to everyone). Facebook has many of the conveniences of YouTube (free and easy). The video is compressed as it is on YouTube, but the quality is better. A disadvantage of Facebook, is that although videos may be specified as available to everyone, they are only available to Facebook members. An advantage of Facebook is that once the videos are played, there is no attempt to redirect the user to other movies. Also, because of the Facebook's user-preferences for distribution of content, there is greater control on who sees the video. Like the other services, Facebook limits the length of videos which can be posted to 20 minutes and under 1GB of total space.

There are also social network sites that are designed for ministries and Christian material. Cross.tv and Tangle.com are just a few social networking sites that offer a dedicated format for building a social network and sharing media to those of like faith.

Podcasts are audio and/or video recordings that are posted on the Websites of those who create them. Podcasts are available through services such as the iTunes music store, or may be downloaded by any other RSS (Really Simple Syndication) client. Getting a podcast listed in the iTunes music store, is a little more involved than creating the podcast, but it is not difficult. It requires the creation of an RSS file describing the podcast. Instructions are found within iTunes (click on iTunes Store, Podcasts, and Submit a Podcast). Although Podcasts are available in the iTunes store, they are available at no cost. A number of Websites such as podomatic.com and mypodcast.com make the process of placing the podcast in the iTunes directory much simpler.

Live365 is a service for those who wish to create their own radio stations to broadcast their own content. Depending on the size of storage space needed, Live365 offers a number of different broadcasting accounts starting as low as $5.95 per month for 200 MB of storage to $99.95 per month for 6,000 MB of storage. They also offer custom broadcasting packages that are priced based on the features selected. Live365's lower cost options interject advertising regularly and/or limit the number of simultaneous listeners, while those that are paid on a monthly basis have no advertising and are permitted a greater number of listeners. With Live365, you upload your files to their service and create a playlist. They will stream your music to any listeners who tune in. The biggest concern with Live365 is building your audience.

Dimdim and **WizIQ** are services designed for free online classes. They are useful to churches, however, because they permit people to join a broadcast at no cost. Once an account is created with these services, setting up a live broadcast for remote visitors is simple. With Dimdim, you log into your account and click "Host meeting." Visitors may join you by clicking on a link (the same every week) to your broadcast. The free version of Dimdim permits up to 20 viewers. A one-year subscription for $99 permits up to 100 viewers. Additional licensing levels are available. WizIQ has similar limitations but does offer up to 500 attendees for a two-hour class at no cost. Upgrading to a premium membership will allow the class lengths to be longer and unlimited recordings and downloads.

SHOUTcast, **Flash Media Server** and **QuickTime Streaming Server** are programs which can run on a computer for those wishing to broadcast live to a wider audience. These programs require a bit more expertise to setup and run, but are quite approachable to a network computer person. The most recommended setup is to pay a site to distribute the stream for the viewers. This lessens the bandwidth requirements for the host. By paying a site the host only has to stream to that site. The site, having adequate bandwidth, can then send the stream to simultaneous viewers.

There are some free video streaming sites which do offer some advertising in exchange for their free services. Ustream.tv and stickam.com are a couple of good sites to use for testing the viability of streaming.

The number of media team ministries required to support the broadcast ministry will be determined by a number of factors, such as:

- Is the broadcast live or prerecorded?
- Is the broadcast to be a "talking head," one camera broadcast, or will the broadcast incorporate shots from different cameras and angles?

VOLUNTEERS

Video Producer—In live broadcast, this person typically receives signals from a number of cameras into a video mixing board and chooses which signal to broadcast (or record). He also directs the camera operators in how to frame shots, when to zoom and when to hold.

Computer Operator—This person could be used to edit video for broadcast, or in the case of live broadcast, operate the computer that sends the signal to be broadcast.

Signal Routing—In live broadcast, this person would troubleshoot any technical issues especially related to lost signals.

Server Maintenance—In a high-end Internet broadcast, a dedicated video server receives the signal from the broadcast computer and distributes that signal to the world. This person would setup and maintain the server. Typically, once this computer is setup, it will run without problem, so this may be a temporary or one-time position, with phone support. Even so it is a good idea to restart a computer functioning as a server from time to time.

CHECKLIST FOR EDITING AND PREPARING RECORDINGS FOR BROADCAST AND INTERNET STREAMING

Depending on how the media team is organized, the editing and preparation of the recording for broadcast could be done by the person doing the recording, or it could be someone to whom audio or video files are provided. Regardless, duties of this person might include the following:

- Start by opening the files containing audio and/or video for the service in the software selected for editing. The files being opened should normally be in a high quality format with little or no compression. The need for high-quality, uncompressed files at this point is to preserve quality as edits are made. If compressed files are opened, edited, then compressed again, then the quality will suffer.

- Add any introductory materials used in the broadcast (introductory splash audio or video, present the title screen or announce the title of the program, introductory theme music, introductory welcome to the service announcements). Those using iMovie or other video editing programs with loops will be aware of the large number of introductory and closing themes available. The presence of these loops in the program makes creating a familiar entrance and exit easy. It is equally easy though to incorporate original music into programs that don't have built-in loops. These introductory and closing musical materials should be short and uplifting. They often set the mood for the broadcast that is to follow. Be sure to update any dates or other time sensitive information in the broadcast. Be sure to affix copyright notices for the church. Although you would think that unrestricted distribution of these materials would be to the greatest benefit for advancing the kingdom of Christ, there are plenty of people who will take materials which are not copyrighted and reuse them in non-flattering ways. It is best to affix a copyright notice. According to U. S. copyright law, a copyright exists as soon as a work is affixed in a permanent media. Registering the copyright is optional, but would be required before seeking legal action against anyone violating the copyright notice.
- Add any exiting materials used in the broadcast (closing splash audio or video, present the farewell screen or announce the title of the program, exiting theme music, exiting farewell announcements, credits). It is fairly common to reserve a closing word for the speaker, especially if substantial portions of his or message was removed for time constraints.
- Scan through the track and remove any materials that may be copyrighted and/or not permitted in the licensing for broadcast. One of the biggest concerns in broadcasting a service is making sure that nothing goes out that might make the church liable for copyright infringement or unanticipated royalty payments. Consequently all music used in the broadcast should be under the terms of any existing licenses the church holds, or should be original

music composed and recorded by the church. Most churches have songwriters in their midst. Often these individuals are happy to donate their efforts (it can create a tax deduction for them); or to sell their songs to their church at a discount. By using original material, the church is generally assured that no copyright violations are occurring. It pays to know the term of any licenses that are held with CCLI, ASCAP, BMI, SESAC, Harry Fox, or other agencies. This will help keep the church out of legal trouble, and will not unduly limit the use of materials used in the service.

- Scan through the track and remove any information or presentations that may be sensitive For example, nothing should be broadcast that would endanger a missionary serving in a country where Christians are persecuted. It may be good to rebroadcast previous services when these kinds of programs are scheduled in the local church. For anything going out for broadcast, checking and double checking is essential. The time crunch of getting it done must not intrude into the quality of the process.

- Scan through the track and remove any obvious misstatements or awkward or embarrassing materials. All individuals involved in the service should be treated with respect. Humor is okay, but good judgment will help identify things which should not be broadcast. Again, double checking anything that goes out for broadcast is essential.

- Identify anyone whose picture was taken during the service and confirm that permission has been granted for broadcast, or replace with a broad shot of the speaker. Permission must be obtained to publish any person's photograph or movie.

- Convert any files to a format appropriate for broadcast. When posting video to the church's Website, I prefer to use embedded .mov files (See the Web section for details on how to do this). The greatest success that I have had with YouTube and such sites is by uploading AVI versions of the video. This video is based on an older standard with little compression so the file sizes are quite large. YouTube will compress the video before it is displayed, but it will correctly understand it.

- Save the program onto any necessary media required for broadcast. Any local television or radio station, or cable television station will have specific requirements for media which they broadcast. Although they can typically work with any format, someone on their end may have to convert it. If you are a regular, they will probably ask for the video in a specific format to eliminate this extra processing on their end. There are a great number of practices among local radio stations and some of their equipment is not standard consumer-issue. Broadcasting with them may require the purchase of some professional equipment.

CHAPTER 9

Web Pages

Churches are finding that it is common for visitors to have perused their Web page prior to attending. The church's Web page is often the first point-of-contact that a person has with the church and may be responsible for that critical "first impression" on a potential church member. Maintaining a current and professional Website helps the church in its outreach and ministry. While churches may maintain Websites through many means, the roles described below will certainly be a part of the Web ministry. As with any media ministry, it is possible that the jobs below may be accomplished by one person, or spread between many.

VOLUNTEER POSITIONS/ROLES

Webmaster—This person oversees the entire Website. They are the contact person for any questions or concerns. This person typically has technical skills and oversees the purchase of Web services, or if applicable, the administration of Web servers. This person will be the one who looks for Web services which can be added to the site (calendars, etc.).

Web Trainer—All staff and pastors will likely have some Web responsibilities such as updating the text reports on their page. It will be necessary for these individuals to be trained to do that.

Writer—A healthy Web ministry requires writers who are committed to frequent updates. While frequent ministry reports can be expected from the various departments in the church, many of the activities of the church will need to be announced, promoted, and reported by the writers on the Website team. If there are writers who are active as a part of a bulletin or newsletter ministry, they can share materials with the Web ministry. Establishing a healthy flow of information to the Web team is essential for maintaining an online presence which reflects the current activities of the church.

Photographer—The Internet is a graphically intense medium. People expect to see pictures when they visit a Website. A photographer who attends and photographs ministry events is essential for the healthy Web ministry. If there are photographers who are active as a part of a bulletin or newsletter ministry, they can share materials with the Web ministry.

HOW TO DO IT

A number of options are available when it comes to creating a Website for a church. Many denominations provide free Websites to their churches (http:// www.ag.org), and some services provide free Web pages for churches (http:// www.housesofworship.com). These services are useful in that they provide templates into which information can be quickly entered. The templates often provide the fastest and easiest means of Website development, especially for churches that do not have individuals with Web-development skills. Some denominationally-provided sites provide easy links to the denomination's missionaries, and other denominational initiatives. The commonly available templates are recommended for churches which do not have individuals with Web-development skills.

Any template-based system, however, is likely to provide limited flexibility. For example, some denominationally-provided solutions prevent the church's site from including META tags which might help Web visitors find the site. Some limit the amount of storage available; some make linking to an existing page on the Website difficult or impossible; some make it impossible to incorporate JavaScript or other innovative Web technologies into the site.

For those churches with a person with Web development skills, a custom Website is usually an excellent idea. The remainder of this chapter will present information needed to maintain a custom Website, but much of the information will be useful to those using template systems also.

WHAT DOES IT TAKE TO POST A WEBSITE?

Domain Name Registration

First, an Internet address (domain name) must be obtained. This address can be anything which is not currently in use. Many churches go with names such as christchurch.org, but many of the shorter names are already taken. To see what is available, go to a domain name registration site such as http://godaddy.com or http://register.com. It is desirable to get as short a Web address as possible, and to avoid the use of things that are difficult to remember. The Web address http://www.grace610495270.com, for example, would be a poor choice. A much better choice might be graceagpa.org (Grace Assembly of God, Pennsylvania).

The question arises, should you purchase a .org or .com address. Churches typically use .org to indicate their status as a tax exempt organization. However, when possible, you want to purchase both. Most people are more acquainted with typing .com at the end of their Web addresses. If you don't own both, anything else could show up on that site for your members to see when they type the wrong extension. Domain name registration is inexpensive, so owning both is recommended.

Server Storage Space

Internet pages are stored on a special computer called an HTML server. (HTML stands for hyper-text markup language and is the universal format of files distributed on the Internet). There are a number of different price plans based on how much space (hard-drive space on the server) and bandwidth (how much is downloaded). If you are uncertain, here's a quick rule of thumb. If you are only using the Web page for text and pictures and have a medium size church, you can go with one of the plans with a limited amount of storage and bandwidth. If you are going to be storing video and audio recordings of sermons and you anticipate a good number of visitors will be downloading these, you should select a plan with unlimited storage and bandwidth. The price will be more, but not much. Frequently server space is available from the same companies that sell domain name registrations and it simplifies life if both domain name registration and server storage services can be provided by the same company.

WHAT SOFTWARE SHOULD BE USED TO CREATE AND MAINTAIN A WEB PAGE?

There are a number of Web-editing programs which can be used to create custom Web pages, and listed below are a few of the more popular options:

Microsoft Word—Simple pages can be created with a word processor like Microsoft Word. It is suggested, however, that a tool devoted specifically to the creation of Web pages is used for several reasons. First, Microsoft Word, is first and foremost, a word processor. Although its basic Web features are well implemented, it is not as capable as a fully devoted Web program. Many of the word-processing features which people use in documents created while in word-processing mode, don't translate well when saved as a Web page. Its advanced Web features are sometimes difficult to find, and it organizes folders according to a scheme which may or may not work well with some Internet servers. Finally, Microsoft Word does not impose any prohibitions on the use of file names. This would be recommended because many Web servers will fail when attempting to send files which have spaces or symbols other than alphanumeric characters in their file names. Web servers are more restrictive with their file names because they often use operating systems other than those created by Microsoft and Apple.

Seamonkey (formerly Mozilla, formerly Netscape Communicator)—This program is a free, open-source Web editor which can be downloaded from http://www.mozilla.com. It is available for Windows and Macintosh computers and operates much like a word processor. Using the basic editing features of Seamonkey, it would be difficult to create something that would not look similar on every browser that views it's pages. Every Web page should be viewed in a number of Web browsers on different computing platforms (Windows and Macintosh) to determine if it displays properly. Unlike word processing which permits exact placement of items on a page, Web pages may only specify approximate placement. A Web page developed for a large monitor, therefore, may not look good on a smaller monitor (or PDA screen).

Dreamweaver—This program is part of the Adobe suite of Web publications. Adobe makes other Web-standard programs including Acrobat and Flash.

FrontPage—This product is by Microsoft and does a good job. It has some features which can only be used when its pages are uploaded to a Web server supporting FrontPage extensions.

iWeb—This product by Apple comes free with every current Macintosh computer. For those that purchase Apple's MobileMe service, creating a Web page is as simple as going to the file menu and choosing publish. Web pages can be published to a folder for use on Web servers other than MobileMe. Some features can only be used when its pages are uploaded to a MobileMe account.

A BRIEF DISCUSSION OF FILE TYPES

When working with Web pages, it is important to use files that will display in all Web browsers and platforms. The most important file types are covered below.

Text

HTML—Hyper-Text Markup Language is the universal format of Web pages. HTML files contain the code for the webpage including viewable text, links to images/media and to other pages/websites, but also contain formatting instructions (how big a font, what color, etc.) and instructions to incorporate graphic and other media files at various points. Because HTML may be viewed by any number of browsers on any number of computers with various size monitors and running virtually any operating system, the exact placement of many of these items is approximate. It is important to test HTML files on a variety of computers and browsers to be sure they display correctly.

PDF—Portable Document Format is a format defined by Adobe Systems in its product, Adobe Acrobat. PDF files contain exact formatting information about text, fonts, graphics and other media items. PDF files can only be viewed by Acrobat Reader or an equivalent reader (Preview on Macintosh). Acrobat Reader is a free download for every computer and platform. You will find it at http://www.adobe.com/.

Images

GIF—Graphic Interchange Format was created by CompuServe, one of the early network providers in the modem age. GIF is a bit-mapped format which supports 256 colors and the inclusion of multiple frames of images (animations). It is well used for black and white documents such as music notation, and for graphics with just a few colors such as cartoons. Its animation is supported universally and is the easiest way to create frame, by frame animation on the Internet. GIF files may contain compression but no loss of data occurs upon reconstruction.

JPG or JPEG—Joint Photographic Expert Group defined this standard. It is the format supported by virtually every digital camera. It supports millions of colors. It may be saved with or without compression. When compression is applied, some data is lost upon reconstruction, but it is generally undetectable to the human eye. JPG files should not repeatedly be edited and saved in a compressed format as the lost data increases each time.

PNG—Portable Network Graphic was designed to replace GIF images. It boasts lossless data compression and supports 24-bit RBG colors & grayscale images. The image format also supports transparency where a background pattern or color behind the image can be seen behind the transparency portions of the graphic.

Music

AIF—Audio Interchange Format was created by Apple and supports a number of compressed and uncompressed audio formats. Its most common use is to preserve the quality of uncompressed recordings of music. It is playable on Windows computers using QuickTime Player (free from http://www.quicktime.com). Because of the large size of uncompressed AIF files, they are seldom uploaded to the Internet.

WAV—The WAV file format was created by Microsoft and supports a number of compressed and uncompressed audio formats. WAV files are playable on Windows and Macintosh computers but because of their large size seldom uploaded to the Internet.

MP3—An MP3 is a sound file which contains strong compression yet produces good quality audio. MP3 files may be up to 10 times smaller than an equivalent uncompressed AIF or WAV file. Because of the way the compression is applied, some data is lost. The reconstructed file is different from the original uncompressed file. Still, many people cannot tell the difference between an MP3 and the original. Even so, it is not a good idea to repeatedly uncompress and edit an MP3 file, because the loss of data compounds.

AAC, MP4—A high-quality but highly compressed sound file used by iTunes.

Video

MOV—Apple QuickTime's standard video format is MOV. QuickTime is free for every computer and platform (http://www.quicktime.com). QuickTime supports a number of compressed and uncompressed formats, but all can be played by QuickTime Player. QuickTime is the format created by Apple products such as iMovie.

WMV—Windows Media Video is the format created by Microsoft products such as Windows Movie Maker. WMV can be played on every computer and platform by Windows Media Player (Macintosh users may have to also download Flip4Mac, and/or Perian to support some compressed WMV files). WMV supports a number of compressed and uncompressed formats. When creating Web files, it is generally necessary to compress video files.

FLV—Flash Video—created by Adobe products and playable by computers with a recent installation of the Flash Web-browser plug-in.

CHECKLIST

- Create a simple Web interface that permits visitors to quickly find things. You can anticipate that certain items on the churches Website will be priorities for visitors and should be quickly accessible from any page. Directions to the church, service times, and contact information will be a priority for first-time visitors.
- Items such as addresses, directions, and contact information should be available on every page (click to see). First-time and returning visitors will find these useful.
- Each ministry of the church should be described with a list of current events and photographs from recent events. The list of current events shows that the church has an active and vibrant ministry.
- The Web page should be registered with search engines and embedded with META tags that help bring it to the attention of those searching for it. See the section below on how to do this. This is not possible with all sites.
- Permissions to post photographs of individuals should be obtained prior to posting them. Some churches create a form that they ask families in the church to sign, especially if they will be broadcasting their services, or if they will be placing recordings of the services on the Web.
- The churches services should be uploaded for broadcast weekly. This is easily accomplished by converting the message into a MP3 file, uploading to the Web host and creating a link on the Web page to the MP3 file.

- The churches publications (newsletters, bulletins, etc.) should be prepared for the Web and uploaded weekly. Typically these will be saved as PDF files and uploaded to the Web. Sometimes, PDF files are not easily accessible on the file, so portions (or all) of the documents will be converted to HTML and published on the Website.
- The church's calendar should be published weekly. This may be a responsibility that is easily assumed by the church secretary or whoever keeps the official church calendar. This person may need to be trained to do this.
- The Webmaster may have the responsibility for managing and maintaining e-mail accounts (pastor@mychurch.com). Normally when a domain name and server space are purchased, the ability to maintain a number of e-mail accounts is granted. Administration is simple: login, create the account, set a password, and train the user to use their e-mail account.
- The Webmaster may have the responsibility for maintaining forms for the submission of various information (applications for special events, request for information, etc.). Creating forms may require some server-side programming, or the server provider may have a simple means of doing this. It is easy to create mailto: forms that send an e-mail to a designated individual every time a form is submitted.
- The Webmaster may have the responsibility for setting up e-commerce functions (donations to the church, etc.). Most Internet service providers make this easy to accomplish. The church may need a "business" or at least a "PayPal" account to do this. It is recommended that churches contact their bank about these services.
- The Webmaster may have the responsibility for the maintenance of private or protected data which is made available to the pastoral staff (membership database, etc.). It is possible to maintain a private church directory online which is only accessible by password to members. This should be hosted on a secure server which can be indicated by a lock icon which appears in the Web browser when visiting the page.

META TAGS

See the brief code excerpt below. Add the underlined line to your Web page in the page header as shown below. Update the keywords for your church's Web page.

```
<html>
<head>
<meta content="text/html;charset=ISO-8859-1" http-equiv="Content-Type">
<META NAME="DESCRIPTION" CONTENT="Grace Assembly of God Church
Homepage, Spring City, Pennsylvania">
<META NAME="KEYWORDS"
CONTENT="Grace,Assembly,God,Church,Homepage,Spring,City,Pennsylvania">
<title>Grace Assembly of God, Spring City, Pennsylvania</title>
</head>
<body>
<br>
</body>
</html>
```

BROADCASTING AUDIO OR VIDEO

The Internet provides a simple means of broadcasting audio and video copies of the service. Some quick details on creating a clean interface for audio and video broadcasts and for creating podcasts are found below. Before proceeding, be sure to read the copyright and licensing considerations in the chapters on recording audio and video. Whenever there is a copyright question, the easiest way to stay within the law is to eliminate the possible offending material from that which is broadcast via the Internet.

There are many ways to incorporate audio and video on a Web page. One of the simplest is to upload the audio or video recording to the Web server and then create a link to the file from one of the church's Web pages:

Embedding a movie is easily accomplished. If the movie is saved on YouTube, there is code on the page that can be copied and pasted as a hypertext snippet into your Web editor that will embed the movie. If the movie is a QuickTime movie, it can be embedded as follows. Insert the following hypertext snippet into your Web editor where you want the movie to appear:

> *<embed src="servicenameanddate.mov" height=16 width=160 autostart=false loop=false>*

Of course, it will be necessary to replace "servicenameanddate.mov" with the filename of your audio or video file, the height and width of the movie with the values for your movie, and your preference on whether the movie should start playing automatically or not. The values shown for height and width work well for audio files. For video files, you should use the width of the actual video, and use the actual height plus 16 to make room for the play bar.

TROUBLESHOOTING

Everybody Thinks They Can Create a Better Web Page

Great! This is a helper in the Web ministry. Engage these individuals as much as possible. If they are ready, give them responsibility for a portion of the church's Web page. You can decide if they should have login information or go through you (probably best to go through you until they have proven themselves).

There Are No (fill in blank) on the Web Page

If the request is reasonable, place it on the Web page. There may be some good reasons to not put up some items (like a guest book, or prayer requests—unless posts are monitored before they go up).

The Web Page Isn't Current

It will be difficult to keep pictures from the latest events on the page, the most current announcements, and the most current calendar events. It will be necessary to give this ministry a great deal of time. Keeping the Web page up to date will also help with search engine rankings such as Bing, Google and Yahoo. The search engines not only look at the meta tags, but even more at the frequency of the updates.

HOW TO USE YOUR WEB PAGE AS AN OUTREACH

- Place the plan of salvation and sinners prayer on the Web page.
- Post a "Verse of the Day" to the Website.
- Post a link to "Devotions."
- Post a link to the Proverb of the day (31 chapters—one for each day of the month)
- Post a lint to the Psalm of the day (150—Five Psalms a day, all in one month)
- Post a link to a plan for reading the Bible in a Year. Link to today's reading.
- Post a link to the Bible and Bible search features.

CHAPTER 10

Computer Networks

Computer networks permit the sharing of resources and information within the church, and through the Internet with the rest of the world. The church has a need for volunteers or professionals who can setup and maintain computer networks, wireless networks, network disks, printers, servers, Web monitoring software, etc. The number of options which are possible now on both the local and world-wide level are increasing.

LOCAL NETWORK

Local network services can be configured so that all staff members share the same printer, scanner and other devices. Every staff member can have their own private network drive. For the easy exchange of information, a public or shared drive can be created which permits staff members to quickly exchange large files. For example, a secretary may ask all staff members to post their articles for the church newsletter or bulletin in a folder on the public drive each week. Because churches have some information which is highly confidential (for example, giving statements and records of personal counseling sessions) it is important that the necessary steps that are taken to protect that information. Because all of this information is available locally, it is accessible through the church's computer network.

HOW IT'S DONE

The means of connecting to these services may be through a wired or wireless network, or combination of both. Typically a church purchases Internet services from a broadband Internet service provider. That company runs a line into the church using phone, cable, or network wires. That line is usually connected to a cable/phone modem or networking device from the company which isolates much of the network traffic in the building from the rest of the Internet service provider's network. The church then runs wires from that device to a wired or wireless router which distributes Internet connections to the rest of the church. The router used at that point may be configured with a firewall which can further protect those within the church from threats from the Internet, block certain outgoing connections and even provide protection from spam, viruses and spyware. The wireless routers can be configured with passwords and security options also so that only those who have permission to be on the network are permitted. All machines within the church which are connected to a single router have some awareness of the other devices on that network. It is through these connections that printers and other devices can be shared. Often, a dedicated computer (server) will be connected to the router to provide other services to those plugged into the network. The dedicated computer may run a special operating system which includes sophisticated serving functions. Even if the machine is only running a basic installation of the Windows or the Macintosh operating system, however, it can offer shared public and private drives.

Adding a Network Printer or Scanner

A network printer is usually connected to the network by plugging in an Ethernet cable which is connected to the router serving the rest of the building. A printer is added to each staff member's computer using the appropriate control panels. It may be necessary to download and install drivers for the shared printer on the computer which will be using it. Scanners are connected and configured in much the same way. They are plugged into the network, and they can be used from computers on the network. These computers may need to have drivers and scanning software installed. Many modern copy machines function as network printers, scanners and fax machines.

Adding a Public or Private Network Drive

Public and private drives are maintained by a "server" on the network. Setting up network drives will require changing some settings on the server. Typically the process for setting up private folders is as follows:

- On the church server, create a user account with a username and password for each staff member.
- Create a folder on the church server for each staff member.
- Set the security preferences for that folder so that it may be read and written by only that staff member.
- Teach the staff member how to log into and use their private folder.

The process for creating a public folder is much the same.

- Create a public folder to be shared by staff members.
- Set the security preferences for that folder so that each of the staff members may read and write to it.
- Show the staff members how to log into and use the pubic folder. Be certain they understand the difference between the public folder and their private folder.

In this process, you may have to use the accounts or users control panel, the sharing or network control panel, and right click (control-click for Macintosh users) the various folders to set who has permission to read and write to each folder. Normally Macintosh and Windows computers can share folders with one another over a network, but this works best when everyone, including the server, has the most recent software.

SERVER-BASED APPLICATIONS

Many churches maintain church attendance and giving records in a database which runs on a local server. Server-based applications typically allow anyone on the network to use the application from any machine. Additionally, some documents can be made available to multiple users (although usually just for reading—only one person can edit them at a time).

WORLD WIDE NETWORK

Even a basic installation of Windows or the Macintosh operating system on a server can permit that machine to operate as a world-wide Web server for HTML pages and other Internet services. The more powerful server versions of the software offered by these companies permit these machines to provide additional Web services such as e-mail, the creation and maintenance of databases, and streaming broadcasts.

Even so, most churches usually elect to purchase server space on computers maintained by others so they don't have to worry about downtime when their computer may not be working, or a computer on their site being hacked. Materials uploaded to a commercially maintained Web server should normally be only those that are approved for public distribution. In some cases these commercially available services provide secure storage, and in those cases, sensitive information should be placed carefully in those areas. Commercially available servers usually provide e-mail accounts for staff members at the church's domain (for example, yourname@yourchurch.org). Setting up databases (for example, a privately accessible membership list), on a commercial or private server is a fairly easy task, but it does require the installation and configuration of some optional software on the server. Most commercial companies will assist in this process.

HOW IT'S DONE

E-mail

When you purchase Internet server space, you are minimally receiving hard drive storage on a remote computer and a machine which will share those files with anyone who types in their Internet address (it's a number which most people don't know). By registering a domain name (mychurch.org) to point to that Internet address, everyone can easily find these files. Typically the main page in the church's Web site is named index.html and when anyone goes to mychurch.org, the index page automatically loads and they can use the links on that page to find anything that's there. What many people don't realize is that the same company, more often than not, also operates an e-mail server using that domain name. By following the Internet service provider's instructions, you can create e-mail accounts with passwords for each of your staff members. You can use specific names such as BillyGraham@mychurch.org, or general names such as youthpastor@mychurch.org. These e-mail accounts can usually be read using any POP and SMTP e-mail client such as Microsoft Outlook, Apple Mail, or any number of others. Additionally, most Internet service providers make a Web interface available for these e-mail accounts. In a browser, you would typically type something like http://webmail.mychurch.org. Many church staff members already have e-mail accounts they prefer to use, so it is also usually possible to forward any e-mail sent to this address to an existing e-mail account.

Creating a Private Folder

Creating a folder which only certain people can access is straightforward. Most Internet service providers permit you to log into a management account using a username and password they provided. Once that is done, you can set the permissions for each folder on the server. If you designate a folder as private, you can also set up additional usernames and passwords for that folder so others will have access to it.

Creating a Membership Database

Creating a database will require the installation of a PHP or SQL database software on your server. This is such a popular function today, that most

Internet services providers have streamlined the process. Log into your account and navigate to the server options. Indicate that you want to install the database software on the computer. Once you've done that, you'll need to create an interface that permits records to be updated, and searched. Fortunately, most PHP and SQL database programs have already done this. You'll generally copy those to a server folder, access them using the instructions for the database you select, and start entering records. You'll also find that there will be sample code for inserting into your Web page which permits others to search the database. The software may permit you to manage who has access to the database, or you can set the permissions for the folder containing the data so that only those who should see it can do so.

There are also software companies who have developed church management software to run on a local server. They will many times require SQL running on the server but they have already written the code to layout and easily customize. User accounts are also supported to limit certain users to different functions.

Streaming Real-Time Video or Audio

Usually a server is configured to run streaming software such as Shoutcast, Flash Media Server or QuickTime Streaming server. Once the streaming software is running, another computer into which a camera signal (or mixed video) is being sent runs a client program for the broadcasting software on the server. That program takes the incoming signal and directs it to the server, where it is distributed to the world or better yet, distributed to a site which then distributes the signal to the world. It is sometimes possible for the serving software and the capturing software to be run on the same computer.

Conclusion

The goals of this book are to increase the effectiveness of sound, video and media within the church with attention to many of the mechanical details involved in the ministry. Hopefully as a result, the reader will be better able to participate in the ministry of their church, can complete their media duties with greater understanding and with less fear and intimidation, and can catch a vision for expanding their ministry.

One missionary once said, "No borders are ever closed to those who develop media." *Lord, open our eyes to the opportunities! We want to run our race with perseverance, and in a way that reflects your glory.* With a heart for service to Christ our King, the media team plays a large role in shining the spotlight on the good news of salvation through faith in Jesus, the equipping of the saints for ministry, and the changing of lives.

May God lead and guide our efforts!

Glossary

AAC—A compressed audio file format, commonly used by iTunes.

AIF—An audio file format, commonly used on Apple computers.

Analog—A signal generated by a non-digital device. Most audio signals from microphones and instruments begin as analog signals and are converted to digital signals in the recording process.

Aux Send—On a mixing board, an output from a channel that is generally controlled by a volume knob. It is used to for a number of purposes such as sending to an amplifier for a monitor, or sending a signal to an effects processor for reverb or other processing. Some mixers have an Aux Return port into which the signal can be plugged, but many require the use of a separate channel for the signal with effects.

AVI—A generally uncompressed and older video format. It is created by a number of digital cameras and video cameras.

Balanced Lines—In audio systems, lines which use special canceling technology for noise reduction.

Byte—A unit for measuring computer memory which is roughly equivalent to a single alphabetic character.

CCLI—Church Copyright Licensing International. CCLI is an organization which sells various licenses to churches which greatly simplify the royalty collection and distribution of copyrighted materials in churches.

CD—Compact disc. An optical disc on which 650 megabytes of digital audio and data may be stored.

Channel—On a mixing board, the path through which an instrument's signal travels.

Decibels—A unit for measuring the strength of audio signals.

Digital—A manner of encoding information using numbers (digits). It is commonly used to record audio and video signals and other data for more accurate storage, retransmission, and reproduction.

DVD—Digital Video Disc. An optical disc on which 4.5 gigabytes of digital video and data may be stored.

DVI—Digital Video Interface. A protocol for carrying high quality video signals. It is often implemented on computers, video projectors, and high definition television screens. DVI connectors are unique.

Effects—On a mixing board, any number of manipulations of the signal which can be performed on the board, or by dedicated equipment. See page 110 for a comprehensive list and discussion of various effects.

EQ—Equalization. An audio effect in which the strength of various frequencies within the signal may be adjusted. For example, a simple EQ interface may let the user adjust the treble (high-frequency) and bass (low frequency) parts of the signal.

Firewire—A communication protocol by which information is transmitted and received. It is often implemented on computers, external hard drives, and video cameras. Through firewire, movies may be moved from camera to computer, edited, and saved again to the camera. Firewire communications are defined according to an older (400) and newer (800) standard, the primary difference being the speed of the connection. Faster speeds are preferred for devices that move much data at once, for example, hard drives and video cameras. Firewire cables come with a number of configurations including 4, 6, and 8 pins on each end.

FLV—Flash Video. A video format defined by Adobe. It is playable using Adobe Flash plug in. FLV video is used by a number of Internet sites including YouTube.

GB—Gigabyte. Approximately one billion bytes of computer data.

GIF—Graphic Interchange Format. A file format for graphics that was originally created by CompuServe, an early networking company. GIF files may contain up to 256 colors, a transparent color, and animations. GIF files are compressed, but their reconstruction renders them exactly as before their compression. GIF files are useful for black and white drawings, music notation, cartoon-like drawings, and logos.

House Mix—The signal that is sent to the main speakers. All microphones and instrument inputs are combined and balanced using a mixing board. The resulting signal should contain a pleasing and musical blend of those sounds. The house mix may differ from the signal sent to monitors on the platform because those signals are designed to aid a specific player or group of players in their performance.

HTML—Hypertext Markup Language. A file format used to define pages which are displayed on the Internet. HTML pages contain text, formatting instructions, links to graphic, audio, and video files to display within the page, and links to other pages. HTML is an imprecise format in which items displayed may not look the same on every Internet browser. Most HTML pages are written so that they look as good as possible regardless of browser or device that is displaying them.

Impedance—A measure of a device's output. Typically high and low impedance microphones and instruments are used. High impedance signals such as those produced by electronic guitars don't travel as far as low impedance signals. High impedance signals should not be used in cables over 20 feet in length. Low impedance signals such as those sent by XLR microphones may travel greater distances.

Instrument Level—A measure of the strength of an audio signal. It usually refers to a signal like that sent by an electric guitar or electronic bass.

JPG—A file format for graphics that was defined by the Joint Photographic Experts Group (JPEG). Virtually every digital camera saves images in this format. The format may be compressed in varying degrees. The compression scheme is one in which the exact image cannot be exactly reconstructed, but in which the reconstruction is good enough for most purposes. JPEGs support millions of colors and are used for color and grayscale photographs.

KB—Kilobyte. Approximately one thousand bytes of computer data.

Lead—A sound on an electronic keyboard or synthesizer which is rich, and clear. It is useful for playing featured melodies and solos.

LED—Light Emitting Diode. A light often used as an indicator on equipment (on or off). LEDs may be used in combination to communicate alphabetic or graphic information.

Line Level—A measure of the strength of an audio signal. It usually refers to a signal like that sent by an electronic keyboard, CD player or iPod.

MB– Megabyte. Approximately one million bytes of computer data.

Meta Tags—Instructions embedded in an HTML Web page containing information about the page such as keywords and titles.

Mic Level—A measure of the strength of an audio signal. It usually refers to a signal like that sent by an XLR microphone.

MIDI—Musical Instrument Digital Interface. A communication protocol for sending receiving recording musical gestures created by performing on a MIDI-equipped musical instrument. MIDI data typically describes which notes were played, how hard they were attacked, and a few other characteristics of the performance. MIDI recorders permit a number of edits, such as correcting wrong notes in polyphonic recordings and correcting rhythmic errors, which are not possible on the same level in other recording technologies.

Monitor—An on-stage speaker used by a performer to listen to their part, and/or those of other musicians. With instruments such as electric guitar and bass, there is often no acoustic sound, so the players must have a speaker which lets them hear themselves. Musicians must hear their performances to stay in key, in tune, and in rhythm. Musicians must hear others to match the style of the ensemble.

MOV—A file format created by Apple for video. MOV files may be played on Windows and Macintosh computers using most browsers and the QuickTime plug-in, and/or QuickTime player.

MP3—A compressed audio file format which reduces the size of an uncompressed audio file by a factor of ten. MP3 files compress the signal in such a way that some data is lost. Although the original signal cannot be exactly reproduced, the reproduction is of a good quality. Various levels of compression can be applied to MP3 files, and those with the least compression preserve the greatest quality.

MP4—A compressed audio file format, commonly used by iTunes.

Mute—To silence a channel on a mixer, or digital audio recording device.

Network—A collection of wires and electronic connectors and equipment that allow computers and other electronic devices to communicate with one another.

Pad—A sound on an electronic keyboard or synthesizer which is rich, and somewhat indistinct. It is useful for sustained notes or chords and often is used as long string sounds would be.

PDA—Personal Data Assistant. A term for a class of devices, usually handheld, which provide information and sometimes communications.

PDF—A file format created by Adobe for text and graphics. PDF files define exactly where everything should be placed and are useful for distributing documents to be printed. The Apple Macintosh operating system contains a feature for creating PDF files from any document. Windows computers may use a number of utilities to create PDF files. Both Macintosh and Windows computers may use Adobe Acrobat to create PDF files with advanced features such as interactive links and security.

Pickup—A microphone usually specially developed for an instrument. In some cases, as with electric guitars and basses, the pickup is installed on the instrument permanently. In others, as with traditional acoustic instruments, they may attach to the instrument temporarily.

Pink Noise—A signal containing all frequencies commonly used in music. A pink noise generator is frequently used in calibrating the equalization of sound systems.

RCA—When describing a connector, a common two-wire connector used to carry a variety of general purpose signals.

Resolution—The accuracy, especially of a computer screen, projector, or printer.

Reverb—An audio effect in which echoes of varying strength and delay are added to the original signal.

Server—A computer which provides services to other devices on a network. In the case of the world wide Web, a server, provides information such as Web pages to others on the network.

Snake—A set of cables bound into one large cable. A snake is typically used for running signals from a number of input sources such as on a stage, to a mixing board where the signals can be amplified and sent to speakers.

S/PDIF—Sony Philips Digital InterFace. A communication protocol for transferring digital audio from device to device. Its input and output is usually through a single RCA jack. Shielded cables are generally used to carry these signals.

Streaming—A type of Internet broadcast in which audio or video files sent just enough at a time to provide uninterrupted playback. A copy of the audio or video is not created on the target computer.

S Video—A video communication standard. S Video cables use a specially shaped connector and are often found on video equipment such as cameras, video players, and projectors.

TB—Terabyte. Approximately one trillion bytes of computer data.

TRS—Tip, Ring, Sleeve. This is the name of a common audio connector which supports stereo signals. It is commonly used on ¼" cables to connect stereo equipment to inputs on amplifiers or other equipment. It may be used to send a balanced signal from instruments which support them to a mixing board.

TS—Tip Sleeve. A common audio connector which supports mono signals. It is commonly used on ¼" cables which connect electric instruments such as guitars, basses, and keyboards to inputs on amplifiers, direct boxes, or other equipment.

TXT—A file format for text that contains only upper and lower-case alphabetic and numeric characters and selected symbols. No formatting of the data (bold, italics, underlined) is saved in a text file.

Unity—The point on many mixing boards where optimum performance is obtained. It is common on many mixing boards to set the main outputs to unity (0) and to make all adjustments using the channel sliders on the board.

USB—Universal Serial Bus. A communication protocol by which information is transmitted and received. It is often implemented on computers and numerous peripheral devices such as mice, keyboards, printers, and hard drives. USB communications are defined according to an older (1.0) and newer (2.0) standard, the primary difference being the speed of the connection. Faster speeds are preferred for devices that move much data at once, for example, hard drives and video cameras. USB cables come with a number of configurations including a long rectangular shape found on most computers, a large irregular hexagonal shape found on many printers, and a small hexagonal shape found on many digital cameras and hard drives.

VGA—Video Graphics Adapter. A protocol for sending video data, typically from a computer to a monitor or projector. VGA connectors are unique in shape.

VHS—A standard format for recording video to tape.

WAV—An audio file format, commonly used on Windows and Apple computers.

WMV—A video file format, commonly used on Windows computers.

WWW—Word Wide Web. The often used term for the global network known as the Internet.

XLR—A common audio connector which supports balanced mono signals. It is commonly used to connect microphones to mixers or amplifiers.

Index

About the Author

 **Dr. C. Floyd Richmond** is a church musician, music educator, and technology specialist. He has taught in public and private Christian schools and universities since 1980. Since 2002, he has served as a member of the Valley Forge Christian College music faculty. Over the years he has held positions as worship leader, church orchestra director, and choir director. He has attended churches ranging in size from a few families to a few thousand. He is frequently called upon for presentations at worship conferences and retreats, school in-service days, local, state, national and international music conferences.

Dr. Richmond is the author or editor of nine course books on music technology, and is the editor and coauthor of Hal Leonard's *Technology Strategies*, chapter author for Thompson's *Technology Guide for Music Educators*, primary author for Alfred's *Composing Music with Notation*, and co-author for Alfred's *Playing Keyboard, and Sequencing*.

He is the chair of the education and curriculum committee for the Technology Institute for Music Educators (TI:ME), and is active with the Association for Technology in Music Instruction (ATMI). He teaches music technology courses around the country, and in recent years has taught at Ball State University, Boston University, Kent State University, West Chester University, Villanova University, Five Towns College, and Valley Forge Christian College. He is also a songwriter and composer with a number of original worship songs, and travels as a performing musician playing a variety of styles from classical and jazz to contemporary worship.